END-TO-END

SOLVED PROBLEMS

WITH R

A CATALOG OF 26 EXAMPLES
USING STATISTICAL INFERENCE

http://stewr.com

N. M. Radziwill

ISBN-13: 978-0-9969160-2-8
ISBN-10: 0-9969160-2-4

Cover Design: Morgan C. Benton
> On the cover is an ouroboros, the ancient Egyptian symbol of a snake or dragon eating its own tail. It symbolizes introspection, the cycle of creation and destruction, hopes and aspirations, and gaining a deeper understanding of the world around you (e.g. by learning statistics and data science). It is synonymous with Rahu and Ketu, the nodes of the moon, which represent the points at which solar and lunar eclipses occur.

Publisher: Lapis Lucera, San Francisco, California.
1st Edition: August 21, 2017 – celebrating the total solar eclipse across the USA

For a free PDF eBook, please email a copy of your receipt (and preferably, a picture of you and/or your book in a beautiful location!) to the author (nicole.radziwill@gmail.com) with "E2E PDF" in the subject line. You will receive a PDF eBook by email AND your picture might show up on the http://qualityandinnovation.com blog. **Classroom materials including slides, videos, labs, and exams are also available at** http://stewr.com **or by request from instructors.** For information on distribution, bulk sales, or classroom adoptions please contact the author directly with the subject line "E2E BULK ORDER" or on Twitter at @nicoleradziwill.

"Dubious Study" - an XKCD cartoon by Randal Munroe
(https://xkcd.com/1847/)

About the Author

Nicole M. Radziwill

Nicole Radziwill is an Associate Professor at James Madison University (JMU) in Harrisonburg, Virginia in the Department of Integrated Science and Technology (ISAT), where she has worked since 2009. Prior to 2009, she spent nearly a decade hanging out with brilliant astronomers and engineers at the National Radio Astronomy Observatory (NRAO) working on software and systems to make giant radio telescopes work. Her teaching interests include quality, innovation, process improvement, cyber-physical systems, cybersecurity management, predictive analytics, intelligent systems, industrial simulation, technology management, and applied statistics. She has been active in the American Society for Quality (ASQ) since the late 1990's, and in addition to serving as one of ASQ's official "Influential Voices" bloggers at http://qualityandinnovation.com, she was recognized by Quality Progress (ASQ's flagship publication) as one of the society's 40 New Voices of Quality in 2011 and "40 Under 40" in 2016.

Nicole is certified by ASQ as Six Sigma Black Belt (CSSBB) #11952 and Manager of Quality and Organizational Excellence (CMQ/OE) #9583. She was Chair of the ASQ Software Division from 2009 to 2011, and served as a national examiner for the Malcolm Baldrige National Quality Award (MBNQA) in 2009 and 2010 appointed by the National Institute for Standards and Technology (NIST). She has a PhD in Technology Management and Quality Systems from Indiana State University, an MBA from Regis University in Denver, and a BS in Meteorology from Penn State. Nicole is the Editor-in-Chief of *Software Quality Professional*, a peer-reviewed journal that covers quality and improvement in software-intensive systems, including big data, analytics, cybersecurity, artificial intelligence, machine learning, and the Internet of Things (IoT).

Her research uses data science to explore quality systems and innovation in production systems, with a focus on emergent environments for living and learning that incorporate cyber-physical systems, alternative economies, and gift cultures such as Burning Man.

Table of Contents

Preface

When I'm trying to learn something new, I typically rifle through hundreds of web sites and at least ten (or so) books and textbooks. Why? Because I need to see a problem solved from several perspectives before I really understand it. I need to see tangible examples of problems being solved, and detailed step-by-step instructions for how I should approach future problems. I need to solve a few problems on my own, with my own hands and brain. I need to get a firm understanding on the "so what" behind the problem... the social, political, economic, and technological ramifications of the decisions that I will make based on my data.

Unfortunately, it's hard to find resources that hit that Goldilocks spot: enough theory to understand what's going on (and not get in trouble by violating the assumptions of the methods you're trying to apply), coupled with enough practice so that you could perform the same analyses on your own data without too much complication. Too often, there's a giant gap between the-math-that-has-all-the-Greek-letters in it and the actually-how-to-get-this-run-on-your-computer part. Once you do figure things out, you even realize that several of the examples that people post online are wrong, and it's hard to look back and remember which ones you can trust.

My goal in writing any book is to fix all of those problems -- and create a set of notes that will let me turn to my trusted friend, My Past Self, any time I need to analyze certain kinds of processes in the future. This book is a result of one such exercise.

When I wrote Statistics (The Easier Way) in R, my motivation was similar: "Why can't someone just write a book that makes me feel like I have a real live person sitting next to me, who cares about me, who wants me to understand things? Why can't someone document some examples in R (my favorite statistical software package) that actually include all of the steps I need to follow instead of leaving out one or two critical steps that leave me tearfully troubleshooting for hours? Why can't someone write a cookbook that provides just enough statistical theory and formulas so I can understand how the analytical solutions match up with the solutions provided by the statistical software?"

My style is to tell you only what I think you need to know to quickly become productive. I'll provide you with some background, some examples, and an explanation of what each of the commands in R does (and the options you can provide to those commands). I want to give you just enough theory so you know exactly what's going on under the surface, and just enough practice so that you can quickly and easily gain insights from your own data. As a result, this book is NOT intended to be a substitute for a full-length text or course in data science, quality improvement, or Six Sigma!

Each chapter has been written so that you don't need to be a math or statistics or programming ninja to be able to complete the exercises. Rather than trying to impress you with my slick coding skills in R, I have purposefully chosen less elegant but more instructive coding strategies, and I've attempted to show you ALL the lines of code for EVERYTHING that is produced in this book. If you see a cool chart or graph, you can be assured that the exact code to produce that chart or graph is within +/- 1 page. I have been repetitive, on PURPOSE, so you don't have to remember every single detail from previous chapters to get the job done in a later chapter.

I use this book as a supplemental text for an undergraduate course in introductory statistics and data science that I teach. I also use it to help students who have taken classes in lean manufacturing and process improvement, and need to hone their math skills so that they will be prepared to do well on the American Society for Quality (ASQ) Certified Six Sigma Black Belt (CSSBB) exam, and the Association of Technology Management and Applied Engineering (ATMAE) Lean Six Sigma certification exam. The book does not cover all the aspects of the exam, but does cover all the statistics and math that most students find challenging, and is also a valuable resource for applying these methods in practice after you've got that Belt on.

Who This Book Is For

This book was written for my students, but's it for you too, if you are:

- A data scientist who wants to know more about structured problem solving using methods of statistical inference
- A quality professional who needs or wants to understand more about data science
- Anyone interested in learning more about statistical methods, statistical distributions, confidence intervals, and data visualization in R
- Preparing for your Six Sigma Black Belt exam (I'm an ASQ Six Sigma Black Belt too... I've included everything in this book that you'll need for the heavy-duty math portion of your certification exam)
- A smart, business-savvy person who wants to make more data-driven decisions (and doesn't want to invest hundreds or thousands of dollars on statistical software)
- A middle school or high school student who wants to do a science fair project that focuses on quality improvement (really, I think you'll be able to understand this book just fine)

I do not assume that you are a programmer. I also do not assume that you are super smart with either computers or statistics, only that you have the motivation to get some data analysis done with R.

I do assume that you already have R or RStudio installed on your machine, and that you are impatient and just want to figure out how to do some useful stuff so you can start impressing your boss, your teachers, or yourself. (I use regular R most of the time, but I'm planning to move to start using R Notebooks soon.)

I do assume that you have a positive attitude, and that you'd like to learn some statistics and data analysis techniques that you can start using immediately.

This Book Uses R

All of the examples in this book use the R statistical software. You need to download and install the software onto your own machine to be able to use it. Go to the R Project web site at http://www.r-project.org and select the link to "Download R". It will ask you to pick a "CRAN Mirror" so find a site that's geographically close to where you're sitting when you want to install R. (If all of the CRAN Mirrors say "https", go to the bottom and choose "HTTP mirrors" before you move forward.) For example, I live in Virginia so I might choose a Maryland or Ohio site rather than one in Argentina or Belgium. Data has to travel over geographic distances too, so I want all those mysterious bits and bytes to have to travel the shortest possible distance between where they live and MY laptop. That way, they will arrive as quickly as possible.

R is usually very friendly to install. But if you need some help to get the program up and running, here are some useful places to start:

- Installing R on a Mac - https://www.coursera.org/learn/r-programming/lecture/9Aepc/installing-r-on-a-mac

- Installing R on Windows - https://www.coursera.org/learn/r-programming/lecture/3ClUX/installing-r-on-windows

- Installing RStudio on a Mac - https://www.coursera.org/learn/r-programming/lecture/qYDfT/installing-r-studio-mac

- There's even a screencast of me installing R on Windows here: https://drive.google.com/file/d/0B4VN55HxlNvKQlhxaTVxV01CakU/view?usp=sharing

Or, you can try to decipher what's in the official R Installation and Administration manual, which can be found at http://cran.r-project.org/doc/manuals/R-admin.html.

How This Book Is Organized

This book has 2 sections:

- Section 1 explains my 7 Step method for solving statistical inference problems, and describes how those steps can be integrated into research reports.
- Section 2 provides 26 end-to-end solved problems using the 7 Step method!

Conventions Used in This Book

Joy in Repetition

Although I have aimed to keep the text as simple and concise as possible, you may notice that there is substantial repetition between sections. That's for two reasons: 1) to drill the 7 Step approach into your head, and 2) so you can start anywhere in this book, and not have to rely on previous chapters to understand later chapters. The only background you'll need is the introduction section that explains the 7 Step method.

My R Code

Code that you can type directly into R is written in 9-point Courier New, and indented half an inch from the left margin, like this:

```
defect.counts <- c(12,29,18,3,34,4)

names(defect.counts) <- c("Weather","Overslept", "Alarm Failure", "Time
Change","Traffic","Other")

df.defects <- data.frame(defect.counts)
```

The code above *creates a vector of numbers* in the first line, *establishes names* for what each of those numbers means in the next two lines, and *creates a special object called a data frame* in the last line. I had to use a smaller font size for code that you can type into R so that most of my text and output would show up looking decent on the printed page. Design purists, I give you my apologies up front.

Code that I typed into R and the output that code produced is also recorded in 9-point Courier New, *but is not indented.* **This is important because it always has a leading caret** (that's the ">" at the beginning of each line). This caret is the R prompt, which you will see if you are using the R Console that comes with non-enterprise installations of the software. **<u>DO NOT TRY TO TYPE THE CARET AS PART OF YOUR CODE OR YOU WILL GET ERROR MESSAGES.</u>**

Here is an example:

```
> df.defects
               defect.counts
Weather                    12
Overslept                  29
Alarm Failure              18
Time Change                 3
Traffic                    34
Other                       4
```

This means that I typed in the command `df.defects` to see the contents of the data frame that I named "`df.defects`" in R. The rest is what R responded back to me. If I typed in "`> df.defects`" I would get an error message that looked like this:

```
        Error: unexpected '>' in ">"
```

(And for experienced R programmers: YES, I know that some of the R code in here is not optimized, and I know some of my simulations use loops instead of `apply`, and how could I ever possibly do something like that because that's not the best thing to do. You're right. I don't claim to provide elegant code in this book... just readable and/or explained code. I have very good coding hygiene when I don't have to worry about whether students will be able to understand it.)

My R Functions

I also keep many of the utility functions I use frequently on GitHub. You can scan a list of them at `https://github.com/NicoleRadziwill/R-Functions`. The text of these functions is not included in this book, but you can browse through the directory on GitHub to see what's available. All of the functions are called in exactly the same way – you just have to source them from the "raw" location on GitHub. Use the `source` command in R to load functions from GitHub, like this for the `z.test` function:

```
source("https://raw.githubusercontent.com/NicoleRadziwill/R-
Functions/master/ztest.R")
```

Then, just use the function as you would any other function:

```
> z.test(80,112)
$estimate
[1] 0.7142857

$ts.z
NULL

$p.val
NULL

$cint
[1] 0.6306212 0.7979502
```

My Data

I keep the data I used in the examples in this book on GitHub and Google Drive. All data in this book is in **case format**, that is, *one observation per row and one variable per column*. You can see a list of it all at `https://github.com/NicoleRadziwill/Data-for-R-Examples`. For data in CSV format, use `read.csv` and the URL for the *raw* data format on GitHub:

```
> mnms <- read.csv("https://raw.githubusercontent.com/NicoleRadziwill/Data-for-R-
Examples/master/Fall%202016%20M%26Ms.csv")
```

For data in plain text format, use `read.table` and the URL that takes you to the *Raw* data on GitHub, like this:

```
> books <- read.table("https://raw.githubusercontent.com/NicoleRadziwill/Data-for-R-
Examples/master/anova-textbooks.txt",header=TRUE)
```

When lines of code are long and wrap to the next line like this, you should be able to copy the entire statement (without the leading caret), paste it into R, and get it to run. Be careful! Sometimes, lines of code depend on earlier lines of code – if you get red error messages, you may have to re-enter *previous* lines of code to get your current line to execute.

My Dependencies

Some of the examples may use commands from packages that are not installed with base R, e.g. the PropCIs package which helps you construct confidence intervals on proportions. To install a new package, or if R gives you an error message that says a particular function is not found, follow these two steps. Note that there are *no quotation marks* in the `library` command:

```
> install.packages("PropCIs",dependencies=TRUE)
Installing package into 'C:/Users/User/Documents/R/win-library/3.3'
(as 'lib' is unspecified)
--- Please select a CRAN mirror for use in this session ---
trying URL 'http://cran.cnr.berkeley.edu/bin/windows/contrib/3.3/PropCIs_0.2-5.zip'
Content type 'application/zip' length 51995 bytes (50 KB)
downloaded 50 KB

package 'PropCIs' successfully unpacked and MD5 sums checked

The downloaded binary packages are in
        C:\Users\User\AppData\Local\Temp\RtmpAx7XHY\downloaded_packages
> library(PropCIs)
```

Once you install a package, you do not need to re-install it; however, if you want to use that package during your R session, you will need to "wake it up" using `library` before you can use the commands.

My Fonts

Most of the text is written in Calibri 10-point font. R code is in 8-point Courier New. There is no design rationale for these choices beyond informal surveys of my students to find the "most friendly font that isn't Comic Sans."

If You Need Help

R has a fantastic help system that you can access by typing help and the name of the function you want help on in parenthesis, e.g. help("hist"). Use it! In addition, don't discount the utility of Google search as a programming tool. Often, you can cut and paste complete error messages into Google and it will take you to one or more discussions where someone else has had the same problem – and been able to solve it. Whenever my students ask me about an error message they've received, the first thing I do is ask whether they've Googled for the error message yet (or not). Or, if it's the nth time they've asked that question, sometimes I'll be playful and go straight to the "let me Google that for you" web site at http://lmgtfy.com – for example, http://lmgtfy.com/?q=R+help.

How to Contact Me

If I have the time, I am more than happy to address comments and questions about this book, its examples, or problems that you are having working through your own data. I am more likely to have the time to respond to you in between semesters (which means most of December, and May through early August). If you don't hear back from me, it just means that your message fell through the cracks, which happens more often than I would like to admit. **Try again with "E2E" in the subject line**! If I don't have the time to answer or explore your query, I'll let you know.

I also invite you to follow me on Twitter - my ID is **@nicoleradziwill** - but be advised, you will also be getting a lot of tweet spam about severe weather, tornadoes, neurodiversity, solar flares and coronal mass ejections, and Burning Man. (You may like this.) However, there are benefits: if there is ever an interesting planetary configuration or an asteroid that is about to impact Earth, you will be among the first to know. I am a multidisciplinary person and my Twitter feed is too.

Disclaimer

The purpose of this book is *not* to be mathematically elegant, comprehensive, or `tidyverse`-based, but to give you enough of what you need to know to be productive - quickly - without leaving you a statistically naïve button-pusher. I've included links to longer, more extensive proofs in many places if you want to know more about the mathiness underlying everything in this book. I am not a professional statistician or mathematical purist, but a realist who analyzes data almost daily; I want you to be able to analyze your data too.

P1. Randomness, Sampling, and Sampling Strategies

Objective

One of the most fundamental aspects of using inferential statistics to draw conclusions about a population is the concept of *randomness*: to get valid results; you need to make sure you have a *random* sample of cases that's *representative* of the population you want to study. In this chapter, you will learn:

- What randomness really is
- How probability is related to randomness
- The difference between a *sample* and a *population*
- The difference between *sample statistics* and *population parameters*
- What it means to generate a *representative* sample
- Some techniques for collecting random, representative samples, and (hopefully) avoiding common forms of *bias*

What is Randomness?

What does it mean to be *random*? When I ask this question in class, I typically hear things like *when something is haphazard*, or *when something is unplanned or unexpected*, or *when you do something without thinking about it*, or crazy and erratic behavior. When you think about randomness this way, it's kind of overwhelming. How can you possibly get a handle on a process that's so wild and unpredictable?

But there's a more precise definition of randomness in statistics. Because although random events are *individually* not predictable, it's often possible to determine what will happen collectively over many events. For example, every time you roll a fair, six-sided die, you will get a 1, 2, 3, 4, 5, or 6. *Each roll is random, because you don't know what you're going to get from roll to roll!* But if you roll that die a hundred times or a thousand times, you'll see that the distribution of possible values is uniform; that is, you will roll each number with approximately the same frequency. Don't believe me? Let's try it. You don't have to sit around rolling a die a zillion times though... we can make R do it (using a process called *simulation*).

People are NOT good random number generators. Here's an interesting exercise you can do if you have a group of people available: have them all close their eyes, and select a number from 1 to 4 at random. Tally up the number of people who choose 1, all the people who choose 2, and so on. Then create a bar plot showing the distribution of people who chose each category. (But before you read any further... COLLECT THIS DATA WITH A GROUP OF PEOPLE!! I want you to collect your own data so you can see what happens.)

Let's imagine that we did this in a room with 26 students. Only 2 picked a "1", 5 students picked a "2", another 13 selected "3", and the remaining 6 students chose "4" as their random number. Here's how you can look at the distribution in R. (If you're plotting your data, be sure to change the numbers in the first line.)

```
choices <- c(2,5,13,6)
barplot(choices, ylab="Frequency", names.arg=c(1,2,3,4))
```

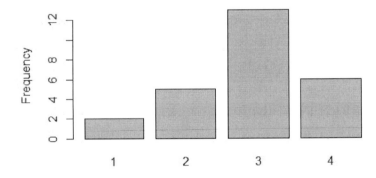

What you'll notice is that *the most frequent value people tend to choose* is a 3. People are hard-wired to favor the numbers slightly above the middle of the possible values, when they're "randomly" selecting on the interval from 1 to 4! One guy decided he was going to test this concept, but instead let people pick between 1 and 20, just to see if the "favoritism to the right of middle" pattern was consistent. What happened? See http://scienceblogs.com/cognitivedaily/2007/02/05/is-17-the-most-random-number/.

I've been doing this test in all of my classes for the past several years, and I think there's only been one time that people did not overwhelmingly "randomly" choose the 3. People are just notoriously bad at generating random numbers, so if you really want to randomize something, you're going to have to enlist the help of a Table of Random Numbers (there are *many* of these online... just Google for one) or a computer program that uses techniques like the Linear Congruential Generator (LCG).

Probability is the *Long Run Relative Frequency* of an Event

What's the probability of flipping a coin and getting heads? You probably intuitive know that it's 50%... because about half the time you'll get heads, and the other half, you'll get tails. But what if you only flip the coin 10 times? Are you going to get exactly 5 heads, and exactly 5 tails? Most likely, no. What if you flip the coin 100 times? How about 1000 or 10000 times? The more times you flip the coin (that is, generate an event) the more likely you will be to observe that the frequency of heads (that is, the number of times that you observe heads) approaches 50%.

Random events are *individually* not predictable (that is, every time we flip the coin, we're never sure whether we'll get a head or a tail) but over a *long run* of many, many, many flips we can be pretty sure that heads will turn up half of the time. As a result, the *probability* of flipping heads is 50% (or, alternatively, 0.5). **The Law of Large Numbers (LLN)** says that when you look at all of your outcomes from a multitude of trials, the results will converge on some expected value - even when the individual outcomes are random.

Samples and Populations

The *population* of all of the possible coin flips that could ever occur, in the history of history, is pretty large. In fact, it's infinitely large, given a universe where you have a lot of time (and coins available to flip). To study the outcomes associated with the random nature of coin flips, we have to choose a *sample* that's smaller than the size of the entire *population* of coin flips.

It would take a really long time to study the entire population of coin flips. Similarly, in a large *population* of people (like all of the people who live in your home country) it would take a long time to study each and every one of those people (a process called a *census*) - but it takes a lot less time and energy to infer things about those people by studying a smaller *sample*. The great benefit of performing statistical inference tests is that they let us get a sense of what happens in a *large population* just by observing outcomes within much *smaller samples*. As a rule, samples are ALWAYS smaller than populations, and your sample size must be selected so that your results will be statistically meaningful.

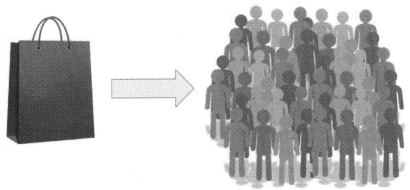

SAMPLE   POPULATION

For many statistical inference tests to work, in addition to making sure your samples are *large enough,* you even have to make sure that your samples are *small enough* – that they contain fewer than 10% of the members of the total population. To make it easier to remember when you're looking at equations, we choose different variable names to represent whether a value is from a sample or from the larger population:

Description	Sample or Population?	Symbol
Mean of a quantitative variable	Sample Statistic	$\bar{x}$
	Population Parameter	μ
Standard deviation of a quantitative variable	Sample Statistic	s
	Population Parameter	σ
Variance of a quantitative variable	Sample Statistic	s^2
	Population Parameter	σ^2
Proportion of an outcome occurring	Sample Statistic	$\hat{p}$
	Population Parameter	p
Proportion of an outcome *not* occurring	Sample Statistic	$\hat{q}$
	Population Parameter	q

If you see a **BAR** or a **HAT** on top of a variable, that's a big clue that you are looking at something measured within a **sample**. The way I remember this is that you can't take everyone in a population *to* a bar, nor can you put a hat on top of everyone's head in a population (it would be too expensive). But you might be able to take everyone in your *sample* to a bar, or put a hat on each person's head in your sample.

Typically, a **bar** also indicates that the variable represents an average of some kind. (If you see a variable with *two bars* on its head, you're dealing with an average *of averages*.) Also, you always refer to the values that pertain to samples as *sample statistics*, and refer to values that pertain to populations as *population parameters*. Remember the alliteration! S goes with S, and P goes with P. *There is no such thing as a sample parameter. There is no such thing as a population statistic.* Also, for the most part, *it's impossible to really KNOW population parameters.* That's why we have to use samples to make guesses about the characteristics of the population parameters.

There's an appendix at the end of this book that shows you how to type letters with bars and hats over them. This is a really useful trick to be familiar with, because there are no fonts that just have x-bar or p-hat natively available. Alternatively, you can use a LaTeX generator like http://www.sciweavers.org/free-online-latex-equation-editor and type \widehat{p} to get a p-hat, or \overline{x} to get an x-bar. (I like to render my symbols using the 18-point Mathpple font using this system.)

A Representative Sample

It's important to select a random sample from a population, but it's equally important to select a *representative* sample. This means that your sample should have characteristics that are similar to those of the entire population. Here's an example. In January 2015, a friend of mine posted to Facebook that the 114th Congress in the United States had just started their work together. He noted that this group was *the most diverse Congress to date* in the United States! 80% were Caucasian, 80% were men, 92% were Christian, 99% were heterosexual, and 50% were millionaires. (Yikes, that's a lot of diversity!)

If we wanted to take a random sample of people in the United States, would selecting the members of the 114th Congress be a good idea? Heck no! Even if we could be sure that we selected these people at random from the population of U.S. citizens, we'd be introducing *bias* into our sample because there are far more people who are not Caucasian, definitely a lot more women, people representing many more religions (or even no religion), people who have different sexual orientations, and... far fewer millionaires. Unfortunately.

The members of the 114th Congress are definitely **not** a *representative* sample of the population of the United States.

Common Sampling Strategies

So now that we know what it means to be random and representative, how do we pick the right people (or things) from a giant population to ensure that we have a nice workable sample to study? Fortunately, there are several approaches you can use. Some are better than others, depending upon the context of your population and the specific 5W/1H for your study. Here are some possibilities:

- **Simple Random Sample (SRS):** In a simple random sample, each member of a population is equally likely to become part of the sample. For example, if I wanted to select a simple random sample of 100 students from the 20,000 students currently enrolled at my University, I would assign each of them a number (from 1 to 20,000) and then use a random number generator to select 100 random numbers. I would survey the students whose numbers matched the ones picked by my random number generator.
- **Systematic Sampling**: This is where you choose every *n*th member that you encounter within the population. In the example above, where we are trying to randomly select 100 students from my University, we would first calculate the *sampling fraction* by taking n=100 and dividing it by the population size. This gives us 0.005, or 1 in 200. We would start with student #200, and then select student #400, and then include every 200th student from there on out to create our sample. A similar (but not as robust) way to do systematic sampling is to select every *n*th person who is a potential candidate for the sample (e.g. every 3rd person who walks by, every 20th item that comes off the manufacturing line, every 5th service call that comes into my company).
- **Stratified Sampling**: Sometimes, SRS and systematic samples don't do a good job at generating a representative sample. In the University case, I might want to make sure that there are enough members from each of the classes (freshmen through graduate students) in my sample. To accommodate this, I would first *stratify* my population into groups, based on those classes, then perform an SRS within each of these groups.

- **Cluster Sampling**: This approach is similar to stratified sampling, but is often more natural when the population is already broken up into different groups. Frequently, the clusters are different physical or geographical areas, organizations, or periods of time. Within each cluster, you generate a simple random sample or a systematic sample, then you combine all the results together to get your full sample. For example, if you wanted to look at differences in study habits between students in the College of Business and the College of Technology, each of those colleges would represent a cluster. If you wanted to study the eating habits of students who live on campus, you might consider each dorm as a cluster, and select a simple random sample from the residents within each of the dorms.

- **Convenience Sampling**: Sometimes, I like to poll my students so we can get some data for in-class examples. I might ask them whether they agree or disagree with a particular political issue, or how many hours of sleep they get each night, or how much money they spend each week on food. Am I getting a random, representative sample of all students at our University? No way. I'm not even really getting a random or representative sample of all of the students in our particular department. But the students are there, in the class, and we need data! Hence the convenience sample. You should be very wary of using a convenience sample to generate any meaningful conclusions. But sometimes, it's all you can get.

- **Voluntary Response Sampling**: When a researcher asks subjects to opt-in to a study, the composition of the sample depends on the people who choose to participate. For opinion polls, you'll tend to get people who feel very strongly (for good or ill) about a particular subject, and you won't hear from people who are basically ambivalent. For studies that require a greater investment of time or energy from the participants, you might only attract people who are available during those days or hours. This can be a problem. Where it's *not* a problem is in situations where you have to find people with a certain characteristic to participate in an experiment: for example, people with a particular disease. If you are running a clinical trial to find out whether a new drug or a new form of therapy is effective, you need to make sure everyone in your sample has that disease. You compensate for the voluntary nature of the participation by ensuring that all of your subjects are randomly assigned into experimental groups, and that they don't know who is receiving the treatment and who is receiving a placebo (or is otherwise in a control group). This is OK as long as you are doing an experiment – which we don't cover in this book.

Preventing Bias

The reason it's important to get as random and representative a sample as possible is that you're trying to avoid *bias*. Bias occurs when your data collection approach systematically favors certain outcomes over others. (Remember the 114th Congress? Clearly, the composition of the members indicates that they *might just possibly* be biased towards decisions that favor white Christian men who are millionaires.)

Sometimes bias can be unintentional. For example, what if you decided to conduct a survey by phone, and obtained a random sample of land-line numbers in your area? There would probably be a lot of older people and senior citizens in your sample (I mean, who do *you* know who still has a land line? Everyone I know uses their mobile as their primary phone number.) Or maybe you've created a survey using Google Forms, and you're going to post it on your Web page so that people can find it and complete it. Your outcomes will be biased towards people who encounter your page, but even more fundamentally, people who have the Internet access in the first place and are *able* to get to your online survey.

Other times, bias can lead to huge embarrassments. During the 1936 presidential election, *Literary Digest* (which was a very popular magazine at the time) published the results of its opinion survey, which predicted that Alfred Landon would win in a landslide over Franklin D. Roosevelt. The magazine had conducted a similar opinion poll for the past several elections, and had correctly identified who the next President would be based on the results. They were noteworthy in that they directly sampled millions of people, and thanks to their accuracy, had earned a lot of credibility!

For the 1936 poll, the *Digest's* sampling strategy involved randomly sampling from phone lists, then sending mailers (which needed to be returned to the *Digest*) asking voters who would receive their vote. But the designers of the survey hadn't considered that at that time, only upper-class and upper-middle-class people even *had* telephones. This was a relatively new technology! And in the first election after the Great Depression, the economy was the key issue for voters, especially for those in the lower and middle classes who overwhelmingly favored Roosevelt. *Literary Digest* ended up with a sample strongly biased in two different ways:

- **Undercoverage**: Because the sampling strategy overwhelmingly favored upper and upper-middle class voters, it was impossible to proportionately include the opinions of voters in other economic classes. Although *Literary Digest* generated a random sample, it was certainly not a representative sample.

- **Non-Response Bias**: Although 10 million people received the mailers, only 2.4 million returned them. As a consequence, the results would be limited to those who felt strongly about participating, or perhaps those who could even afford the postage to return their survey. (Granted, due to the initial selection bias, this latter possibility would be less likely.)

Both of these are forms of **selection bias,** meaning that there's a problem in how the sample was generated. You can also have **voluntary response bias**, in which the participants in your study self-select and typically only engage if they're interested in (or passionate about) what you're investigating.

Something similar happened in the 2016 Presidential election between Democratic contender Hillary Clinton and Republican Donald Trump. Although pre-election polls and exit polls put Clinton firmly in the lead, these polls may have suffered from something called **biased nonresponse**, which means people who decline to participate in a survey are markedly different than those who are willing to participate.

In addition to selection bias, there are other sources of bias that can be attributed to an inadequate measurement process. For example, **response bias** can arise if the questions you ask your survey participants are worded improperly, or lead your respondents to a particular answer. You can also introduce **social desirability bias** by asking questions that people are hesitant to answer, for example, about illegal or embarrassing activities. Bias is always an issue, and it's your job to craft your sampling strategy and design your survey in a way that minimizes it. You'll probably never end up with a sample that's not biased in some small way, so be sure you record your thoughts and state those potential sources of bias when you describe the assumptions and limitations of your study. Convenience samples are *usually* biased; voluntary response samples are *always* biased.

Now What?

Before you actually embark upon selecting your sample, you'll need to determine the proper *sample size* so that your results will be statistically significant. Appendix D, titled "Calculating Appropriate Sample Sizes Using Power Analysis" will help you do this. In the meantime, here are some places you can visit online to learn more about the concepts in this chapter.

- Find out more about biased nonresponse in the 2016 Presidential election at
  https://www.qualtrics.com/blog/biased-nonresponse-polls-missed-2016-election-mistakes/.

- Here's a nice overview of the terms and concepts associated with sampling, prepared by the Web Center for Social Research Methods:
http://www.socialresearchmethods.net/kb/sampterm.php
- One of the best resources I've found to learn more about sampling strategies - and by best, I mean THIS IS ONE OF THE BEST RESOURCES I'VE EVER SEEN IN MY LIFE - is at
http://dissertation.laerd.com/sampling-strategy.php
- More information about the *Literary Digest* story can be found at
http://www.math.upenn.edu/~deturck/m170/wk4/lecture/case1.html
- Wikipedia has a great page on sampling bias at http://en.wikipedia.org/wiki/Sampling_bias
- I also like this article on "Elements of Sampling" because it's written on behalf of a professional society, and illustrates how sampling can have practical applications for real people in their real jobs (in this case, accounting auditors):
http://www.nysscpa.org/cpajournal/2004/1104/essentials/p30.htm

P2. Dr. R's 7 Steps

Objective

In this chapter, you'll learn how to solve every statistical inference problem using the same, simple recipe. Not a statistical chef? No problem! As long as you can read the recipe book, and follow some simple instructions for how to mix and bake your data, you'll do great.

Here's some background. When I was in grad school, I had an excellent professor named Dr. Mike Hayden. He indoctrinated us into his "Hayden's 16 Steps" for doing hypothesis testing, which involved documenting our process and results in a comprehensive way. After I started teaching statistics, I consolidated and streamlined his process into 12 Steps (which felt reminiscent of 12 step addiction recovery programs, adding to the "therapeutic feel" of the approach). When I graduated, I became Dr. Radziwill, which can be hard to pronounce; students tend to shorten it. Several of them pointed out how appropriate it is that "Dr. R is in love with R" so we christened the methodology "Dr. R's 12 Steps."

After teaching the 12 steps for a few years, we found that we relied on seven of the steps for most of our problem-solving, and only used the additional steps when we were writing research reports. Whether we use some steps, or all of the steps, the overall process is the same: 1) **Estimate** the solution, 2) solve **Analytically** using equations, 3) solve the problem **Computationally** using R, and then 4) **Compare** the answers to check your results.

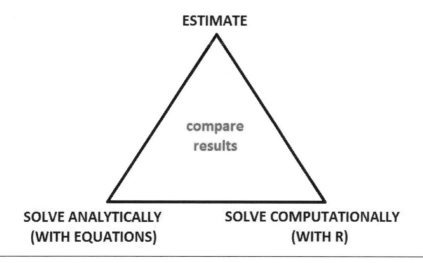

ESTIMATE

compare
results

SOLVE ANALYTICALLY
(WITH EQUATIONS)

SOLVE COMPUTATIONALLY
(WITH R)

The 7 Steps in the Context of a Research Report

The general recipe you will follow starts with **Step 0**, in part because I'm a programmer (we regularly start counting with zero) and in part because if your assumptions don't check out, you can't even more to the first real step of the inference problem. The 7 Steps are performed for *each research question* (RQ), and most research projects have 3-4 RQs.

Abstract – This 200-400 word executive summary briefly describes the problem and why it's important; the methodology, results, and conclusions; and what those conclusions *mean*. A reader should be able to read this part *only* and completely understand everything you did.

I – Introduction: Describe the overall problem and why it's important to solve.

II – Background: Have previous studies been done like this? What did they conclude?

III – Methodology: Describe how you plan to collect your data, what sampling strategy you will use, and what sample size you need to achieve the statistical power you want. List the categorical and quantitative variables you will gather. List your RQs and specify which statistical test you will perform for each one. Briefly state your Null & Alternative Hypotheses so your readers know what's coming next.

IV – Results: Provide some descriptive statistics, with charts, graphs, and tables to give the reader a sense of what the data you collected looks like. Then, for each RQ, execute your problem-solving recipe:

        Step 0: Check Assumptions

        Step 1: Set Null & Alternative Hypotheses

        Step 2: Set α, the Level of Significance

        Step 3: Calculate Test Statistic (T.S.) Analytically

        Step 4: Draw a Picture

        Step 5: Find the P-Value

        Step 6: Draw Conclusion – Is the P-Value < α? If so, Reject the Null

        Step 7: Find the Confidence Interval & Confirm Work in R

V – Discussion and Conclusions: At this point, you have drawn one conclusion for each of your RQs. What did you figure out about your population? How do you explain it to your grandmother? What future research *could* you do now?

References – Include your sources in APA format, which you can get from Google Scholar.

Tips for the Introduction and Background Sections

In the introduction, frame your problem and get the reader interested in it:

- What's this project all about? Why did you decide to do this project, why is it interesting, and *to whom* is it interesting?
- State one or more substantive research question(s) that can be investigated by the technique focused on in the assignment. Remember that a question ends in a question mark. (A problem statement is not a statement of what you plan to do! "I am going to..." is not a problem.)
- The background section usually contains a *literature review*. Most students think this means "find some web pages that give general information about your topic and list them in the reference section" which is unfortunately incorrect. Your job in describing the background is to figure out *all the people who have studied this problem – or problems similar to it – in the past*. This provides the basis for you to justify that you're doing something new and different, and also gives you a rich landscape of knowledge against which you can compare your results.

Tips for the Methodology Section

In the methodology section, describe everything you did to obtain your results, including:

- The survey questions that you ask your subjects are NOT your research questions.
- Describe the population you're attempting to characterize, the sample you are collecting, and justify the sampling *strategy* you selected based on what you know about the population. Did you use simple random sampling, systematic sampling, cluster sampling, or some other technique?
- Describe how you collected the data, that is, the data collection technique and any *instrumentation* used. Did you collect the data directly, or did you use data that you got from some other source (such as an archive)?
- Describe units and sampling frequency (if appropriate). Describe the scope of your data collection (which is important, for example, if you only collected data on weekends, or only at night, or only during a particular week).
- How many respondents did you sample, and were they people, events, or what? **Most importantly, how did you compute the appropriate sample size?** If you did a power

analysis, explain and justify the trade-offs you considered in terms of Type I Error, Type II Error, and power. (There are power analysis instructions in Appendix D.)

- Did you use someone else's survey? If so, report its reliability and validity.
- List all of the quantitative and categorical variables you collected, being sure to note which variables are *quantitative* and which are *categorical*. Describe recoding or computing schemes that may have been used, for example to transform quantitative variables into categorical variables. If you are *defining* categories based on some external factor (e.g. "honors students are considered to be those with a cumulative GPA of 3.5 or higher") state those definitions as well as a justification for why you split up the categories in that way. If you had to calculate any data based on the raw data you collected, explain it here as well.
- Set your alpha (Type I Error) and explain why this alpha was selected in terms of cost (especially cost of gathering more data), risk (of incurring a Type I or Type II error), and ethical considerations (envisioning if and how the results of your study might be used by other people).

Tips for the Results Section

In the results section, your job is to present the results of your analytical solution (using equations), your computational solution (in R), and compare to make sure they yield the same conclusions. Check to make sure that the conclusion you draw from the confidence interval MATCHES the conclusion you drew from your statistical inference test. You don't have to interpret any of the results; that happens in the final section.

Tips for the Discussion and Conclusions Section

Finally, which null hypotheses did you **reject**? Which null hypotheses did you **fail to reject**? Note that these are the ONLY two conclusions you can draw. You cannot accept a null hypothesis; if you reject the null, you cannot say that you accept the alternative. There's always a chance (due to sampling error) that you're not getting an accurate view of the population at all. This is a game of *disproving*, not proving. Additionally:

- Discuss any important assumptions, limitations, threats to validity or other pertinent factors related to the statistical technique selected. Describe how the assumptions were tested, how you *interpreted* the test of the assumption, and what your choices were for moving forward if all of the assumptions were not met.

- At the very end, provide a summary of the story that *all* of your conclusions present when considered together. **Make it exciting, like Elon Musk does:** https://medium.com/firm-narrative/want-a-better-pitch-watch-this-328b95c2fd0b#.si932sh7l.

Helpful Resources

- Please feel free to use this template for your research report. It refers to chapters in *Statistics (The Easier Way) With R, 2nd Ed.* https://docs.google.com/document/d/1eBvfNJ7-ZimUmpOVF_XVc5NPn6-Vq9KK6chaPXF3VQw/pub
- A project proposal template (which you can drop in to your research report) is here: https://docs.google.com/document/d/1Kzwl_FsefTGcOWf-89UDDxl8a0NzzzV-op4iOAkW40A/edit?usp=sharing

Acknowledgements

- You can find out more about Dr. Mike Hayden, who originally inspired this approach with his 16 Steps, at http://technology.indstate.edu/directory/haydenm.htm

P3. Developing Research Questions (RQs)

Objective

To 1) **construct** well-formed research questions (RQs) that can be explored using various methods for statistical hypothesis testing, and to 2) **deconstruct** research questions to figure out which statistical methodology *should* be used. Note that RQs are much different than survey questions, which you write to obtain each of the variables you collect. An example of a survey question is "What is your age?" An example of an RQ is "Are people who watch TV on a daily basis older than those who do not?"

Background

Fortunately, once you know what variables you plan to collect, putting together research questions is pretty easy - it's just like filling in Mad Libs (which, if you weren't so fortunate to grow up during the days when these were one of the fun things you did at home after school, play with some now before you keep reading at http://www.madlibs.com.) With a properly phrased research question, it's much easier to select the appropriate statistical test to answer it. RQ development is covered for each of these tests:

- One-sample t-test
- Two-sample t-test
- Paired t-test
- One-way Analysis of Variance (ANOVA)
- One proportion z-test
- Two proportion z-test
- Chi-Square Test of Independence
- Linear Regression
- F Test for Equality of Variances

Concepts that are fundamental to this chapter are 1) the difference between *categorical* and *quantitative variables*, and 2) the difference between a *sample* and a *population*. (If you need to, review Chapters 1.3 and 3.1 before proceeding.) Each statistical test requires that you have data: some combination of categorical and quantitative variables. **The types of data you have collected dictate what types of statistical inference tests you can apply.**

Where Do I Begin?

First, pick a <u>topic</u> – any topic you are interested in. I've had students start with all sorts of topics: fishing, skeet shooting, exercising, cooking, cars, plants, animals, knitting, attitudes towards parking, attitudes towards political issues, attitudes towards sex and drugs, computers, computer/app use, food preferences, customer service, cognitive responses, or maybe even improving a particular process.

Next, determine your <u>unit of analysis</u>. In the M&M data referenced earlier in this book, the unit of analysis was one M&M, and we recorded color and defect for each candy. In the weather data used earlier, the unit of analysis was one day. (In other weather data I've analyzed, the unit of analysis was one hour, or one minute.) If you give people a survey, your unit of analysis is a person. If you are improving a process, your unit of analysis might be one run of that process.

Finally, what information could you gather for each of those units of analysis? If you're surveying people, what categorical variables could you collect from them? Similarly, what quantitative variables could you collect from them? <u>Create a list of categorical variables</u> on the left side of your paper, <u>and a list of quantitative variables</u> on the right side of your paper. You don't have to collect them all, but this will help you brainstorm potential RQs.

When you identify an interesting RQ, <u>write down the null hypothesis</u> (which represents what you *think* is happening in the population) and <u>choose one alternative hypothesis</u>.

One-Sample t-test

For this test, you only need <u>ONE quantitative variable</u> measured from your sample. You will compare the measurements you take from your sample with a *standard*, a *target*, or a *recommended value*. For example, the *speed limit of a particular stretch of highway* would be a standard. The typical temperature of the healthy human body is 98.6 degrees F, and the expected value of the boiling point of water is 100 degrees C or 212 degrees F. A recommended value for *how many hours of sleep an adult should get each night* could be 7 hours, but this will depend on who or what is making the recommendation. **Whenever you use a recommended value in your one-sample t-test, be sure to get the recommendation from a valid, reputable source.** (For example, get medical recommendations from journal articles or reputable sources like Centers for Disease Control – references you can cite.)

RQs for the one-sample t-test are phrased like this:

- Is the value of [Quantative Variable] for [Unit of Analysis] [*greater than OR less than OR different than*] [the value of the standard, target, or recommended value for the Quantitative Variable]?
- Do [Unit of Analysis] [meet, exceed, or fall short of the standard, target, or recommended value for the Quantitative Variable], on average?

That means, for this test, there are **three elements** you need to glom together:

Name of a Quantitative Variable	A Sign: >, <. or ≠	Standard, Target, or Recommended Value
Body Temperature	>	98.6 F
Speed	>	25 mph
Length of a Ruler	≠	12.0 in

The three signs *greater than, less than, and different than* represent the three possible alternative hypotheses. Here are some examples with variable names inserted:

- Is the **average body temperature** [Quantitative Variable] of **students on our campus** [Unit of Analysis] greater than **the expected value of 98.6 degrees F for healthy individuals** [Expected Value for the Quantitative Variable]?
- Do **cars on this road** [Unit of Analysis] drive faster than the **posted speed limit** [Standard for the Quantitative Variable]?
- If I work for a company that makes rulers, is the **length of each ruler** equal to the target of exactly **12.0 inches**?
- When I add two tablespoons of salt to my water, does it **boil at a temperature** [Quantitative Variable] greater than **100°C** [Expected Value]?
- Did **students in this class** [Unit of Analysis] do better than **last year's students** [Target for the Quantitative Variable] on **Exam 1**?

		What it means
H$_0$:	μ = 0	There is no difference between the REAL means of this quantitative variable and the standard, typical/expected value, or recommendation we are comparing it to
H$_a$:	μ > 0 (one-tailed)	The REAL mean of this quantitative variable is bigger than the standard, typical/expected value, or recommendation we are comparing it to
	μ < 0 (one-tailed)	The REAL mean of this quantitative variable is less than the standard, typical/expected value, or recommendation we are comparing it to
	μ ≠ 0 (two-tailed)	The REAL mean of this quantitative variable is different than the standard, typical/expected value, or recommendation we are comparing it to (either greater or less than... doesn't matter which)

Because this is a t-test, the Test Statistic (T.S.) that you will calculate will be a **t**.

Two-Sample t-test

This test compares the means of a quantitative variable that is observed in each of two groups. For this test, you need <u>at LEAST one categorical AND one quantitative variable</u>:

- Each category will be represented by *one sample each*
- A *single quantitative variable* is measured across cases in both categories

Research questions are of the form:

- Is the average of [Quantitative Variable] [*greater than, less than, different than*] for [Category 1] than it is for [Category 2]?
- Do [entities in Category 1] have [*greater than, less than, different than*] [Quantitative Variable] than [entities in Category 2]?

That means, for this test, there are **three elements** you need to glom together:

Quantitative Variable in Bag 1	A Sign: >, <. or ≠	Quantitative Variable in Bag 2
Product Ratings from women age 30-40	>	Product Ratings from men age 30-40

Mean Time to Failure (MTTF) for Energizer batteries	>	Mean Time to Failure (MTTF) for Duracell batteries
Exam Scores for Summer Students	<	Exam Scores for Spring Students

The three signs *greater than, less than, and different than* represent the three possible alternative hypotheses. Here are some examples with variable names inserted:

- Do **women between the ages of 30-40** [Category 1] provide higher **ratings for our product** [Quantitative Variable] than **men between the ages of 30-40** [Category 2]?
- Do **Energizer batteries** [Category 1] **last longer** [Quantitative Variable] than **Duracell batteries** [Category 2]?
- Is **job satisfaction** [Quantitative Variable] in our organization greater **after the annual company picnic** [Category 1] than **before it** [Category 2]?
- Are **exam scores in our class** [Quantitative Variable] lower for **students who enrolled this summer** [Category 1] than for **students who enrolled last spring** [Category 2]?
- Is the average **number of nights a person drinks each month** [Quantitative Variable] greater for **male students in the College of Business** [Category 1] than it is for **male students in the College of Technology** [Category 2]?
- Did employees remember a greater **number of initiatives from our strategic plan** [Quantitative Variable] **after the new training** we just developed [Category 1], as compared **to before the training** [Category 1]?

		What it means
H_0:	$\mu_1 - \mu_2 = \mu_0$	There is a difference of μ_0 between the REAL means of this quantitative variable in Category 1 and Category 2, often μ_0 is zero
H_a:	$\mu_1 - \mu_2 > \mu_0$ (one-tailed)	The REAL mean of this quantitative variable is bigger for Category 1 than it is for Category 2
	$\mu_1 - \mu_2 < \mu_0$ (one-tailed)	The REAL mean of this quantitative variable is less for Category 1 than it is for Category 2
	$\mu_1 - \mu_2 \neq \mu_0$ (two-tailed)	The REAL mean of this quantitative variable is different in Category 1 than it is for Category 2, but it could be different in EITHER direction (greater than *or* less than)

Because this is a t-test, the Test Statistic (T.S.) that you will calculate will be a **t**.

Paired t-test

This test is JUST like the two-sample t-test, although there's one critical difference: the two samples have to be UNITED by "who" is observed. For this test, you need <u>one quantitative variable *measured at two different times* or *under two different conditions*</u>. This is the "pre-test/post-test" or "before and after" statistical test that tells you whether an improvement occurred from the first administration of the test until the last. Research questions are of the form:

- Is the mean *difference* of the [Quantitative Variable] from the beginning to the end of the evaluation period [*greater than, less than, different*] than zero?
- Did **performance** [Quantitative Variable] improve **from the beginning** of the period **to the end**?

		What it means
H₀:	$\mu_D = D$	There is no difference between the REAL mean-of-the-differences of this quantitative variable and what we anticipated (D; note that D often equals 0)
H_a:	$\mu_D > D$ (one-tailed)	The REAL mean-of-the-differences of this quantitative variable is greater than D
	$\mu_D < D$ (one-tailed)	The REAL mean-of-the-differences of this quantitative variable is less than D
	$\mu_D \neq D$ (two-tailed)	The REAL mean-of-the-difference of this quantitative variable is NOT D but we don't know for sure whether it's on the "greater than" side or the "less than" side

Because this is a t-test, the Test Statistic (T.S.) that you will calculate will be a **t**.

One-way Analysis of Variance (ANOVA)

This is the "one of these things is not like the other" test. For this test, you need <u>one categorical variable and one quantitative variable, and there must be three or more groups that you split your observations into using the categorical variable</u>. The one-way ANOVA is very similar to the two-sample t-test, but instead of comparing the mean of a quantitative variable between only *two* groups, you compare the mean of a quantitative variable between *three or more* groups. So, if you have *n* different groups:

- Each of the *n* categories will be represented by *one sample each*
- A *single quantitative variable* is measured in each of the 3+ categories
- In an experiment, each of the *n* groups can represent different experimental treatments
- Each of the *n* groups can also represent different time periods in which the quantitative variables are measured (e.g. months, or days of the week)

Research questions are of the form:

- Is the average value of [Quantitative Variable] the same [in all *n* Categories]?
- Do [entities in Category 1], [entities in Category 2], or... [entities in Category *n*] report different [Quantitative Variables]?
- Which of the *n* treatments works best to achieve [a particular goal]?
- Was the average [Quantitative Variable] different at any of the *n* time periods when it was measured?

		What it means
H₀:	$\mu_1 = \mu_2 = \mu_3 = ... \mu_n$	All of the n samples (1, 2, 3, etc.) have the same mean
Hₐ:	At least one of the means is different	Not all of the samples have the same mean. However, we can't tell WHICH sample (or samples) are different... we need to do follow-up tests, which are called TESTS OF MULTIPLE COMPARISONS. Or a whole lot of two sample t-tests to compare each of the combinations (which is NOT advised... it will propagate errors *fast*).

Because this is NOT a t-test, the Test Statistic (T.S.) that you will calculate will be an **F**.

One Proportion z-test

This test helps you compare a *proportion* that you have observed in your sample with a *standard or recommended* proportion. Often, the standard or recommended proportion will come from a previous belief or opinion, or a published report or published academic journal article. We test to see whether the observed proportion differs from what we expected.

- Your observed proportion should be the *proportion of successes* you observe within a particular group
- You can define *success* any way you want to!
  - People who *have* a certain characteristic

  o   People who *hold* a certain belief or opinion
  o   People who have *succeeded* in meeting a certain condition, such as winning a game, or *demonstrating a characteristic* within your study

That means, for this test, there are **three elements** you need to glom together:

Observed Proportion	Sign: >, <. or ≠	Standard, Target, or Recommended Value
% of customers who are satisfied	>	0.75
% of students who pass my class	<	0.90
% of defective product	≠	0.08

Research questions are of the form:

• Is the proportion of [subjects who meet a particular condition or are members of a particular category] [*greater than, less than, different than*] [the standard]?

• Do a majority of subjects [meet this particular condition]? Note: If you're testing for majority opinion or majority participation, you will always set your alternative hypothesis to be H_a: $p > 0.50$.

		What it means
H_0:	$p = p_0$	There is no difference between the REAL population proportion p and what we anticipated (p_0)
H_a:	$p > p_0$ (one-tailed)	The REAL population proportion p is greater than what we anticipated (p_0)
	$p < p_0$ (one-tailed)	The REAL population proportion p is less than what we anticipated (p_0)
	$p \neq p_0$ (two-tailed)	The REAL population proportion p is NOT what we anticipated (p_0) but we don't know for sure whether it's on the "greater than" side or the "less than" side

Because this is a z-test, the Test Statistic (T.S.) that you will calculate will be a **z**.

Two Proportion z-test

This test helps you compare *a proportion that you have observed in one group* in your sample, with a *proportion that you have observed in another group* within your sample. Your groups will most likely be determined by a categorical variable that you have acquired in your data collection.

- Your observed proportion for each of the two groups should be the *proportion of successes* you observe within each group
- You can define *success* any way you want to! People who *have* a certain characteristic? People who hold a certain belief or opinion? People who have succeeded in meeting a certain condition, such as winning a game, or *demonstrating* a certain characteristic under the constraints of your study?

That means, for this test, there are **three elements** you need to glom together:

Proportion in Bag 1	Sign: >, <. or ≠	Proportion in Bag 2
% of men who favor a political candidate	>	% women who favor a political candidate
% of defective products this month	>	% of defective products last month
% passing certification this year	≠	% passing certification last year

Research questions are of the form:

- Is the proportion of [subjects who meet a particular condition or are members of a particular category] [*greater than, less than, different*] than the proportion of [subjects who meet a particular condition or are members of a particular category]?
- Is there a difference between the proportion of [subjects who meet one condition] and [subjects who meet another condition]?

		What it means
H_0:	$p_1 - p_2 = p_0$	There is no difference between the two population proportions p_1 and p_2 and what we anticipated (p_0)
H_a:	$p_1 - p_2 > p_0$ (one-tailed)	The difference between the REAL population proportion p_1 and the REAL population proportion p_2 is greater

	than what we anticipated (p_0)
$p_1 - p_2 < p_0$ (one-tailed)	The difference between the REAL population proportion p_1 and the REAL population proportion p_2 is less than what we anticipated (p_0)
$p_1 - p_2 \neq p_0$ (two-tailed)	The difference between the REAL population proportion p_1 and the REAL population proportion p_2 is *different* than what we anticipated (p_0)

Because this is a z-test, the Test Statistic (T.S.) that you will calculate will be a **z**.

Chi-Square Test of Independence

With this test, you are comparing *counts of observations that have been classified according to two categorical variables* to see if they are distributed evenly between all the combinations of categories. If they are not distributed evenly, that indicates that there must be some *relationship* or some *preference* between the variables. But there's no way to tell exactly what that relationship is -- barring further tests! For Chi-Square:

- You need *exactly two* categorical variables
- You should have them arranged in a *contingency table* (that's the one that looks like a bunch of boxes, with values for one categorical variable across the top spanning the columns, and values for the other categorical variable down the left side, spanning the rows) with *counts of observations* tallied up in each cell:

	Male	Female
In favor of that really critical decision	# of men in favor	# of women in favor
Opposed to that really critical decision	# of men opposed	# of women opposed

Research questions take one of two forms, so it is very easy to brainstorm possible RQs that could be solved using the Chi-square test of independence. Just pick *any* two of the categorical variables that you could collect, and plug them into the following sentences to see if any of them would be interesting to investigate:

- Are [Categorical Variable 1] and [Categorical Variable 2] independent?
- Is there a relationship between [Categorical Variable 1] and [Categorical Variable 2]?

		What it means
H_0:	[Categorical Variable 1] and [Categorical Variable 2] are independent.	The counts of your observations have been uniformly distributed across your cells, given the number of observations you made.
H_a:	[Categorical Variable 1] and [Categorical Variable 2] are NOT independent.	The counts of your observations are NOT uniformly distributed across your cells, given the number of observations you made.

Because this is a Chi-square-test, the Test Statistic (T.S.) that you calculate will be a $\chi 2$.

Simple Linear Regression

Linear regression helps you determine whether there is a linear relationship between two quantitative variables. The variables have to be matched based on the unit of analysis so that x is the independent variable, y is the dependent variable, and a scatterplot can be generated from (x, y) points. Research questions are of the form:

- Is there a linear relationship between [Response Variable] and [Independent Variable(s)]?
- Can the [Dependent Variable] be predicted from the [Independent Variable(s)]?
- Does the [Independent Variable] predict the [Dependent Variable]?

		What it means
H_0:	$\beta = 0$	The slope of the regression line is zero (that is, there is no linear relationship between x and y)
H_a:	$\beta \neq 0$	The slope of the regression line is nonzero (that is, there *is* a linear relationship between x and y)

Inference tests can also be performed to see if the slope of a best fit line is significant. In addition, this test for the significance of a regression slopes translates very well to multiple regression: if you are testing a linear model with *multiple potential predictors*, looking at the p-value associated with the slope attached to each predictor can tell you whether that predictor is significant. (These p-values appear on R output from the `lm` command.)

The Test Statistic (T.S.) used for this test is a **t**. You can also test for the significance of the regression *intercept*, in addition to the regression coefficients (slopes).

F Test for Equality (Homogeneity) of Variances

This test helps you compare a *variance* observed in *one group* in your sample, with a variance that you have observed within *another group* within your sample. Your groups will most likely be determined by a categorical variable that you also sampled. Because the test statistic involves the *ratio* between the two variances, if we always put the larger variance in the numerator, then only the one one-tailed alternative makes sense. This test can be used to check assumptions for other tests that require groups with equal variances.

- This test is *very* sensitive to normality. Make sure the observations are normally distributed, using a QQ plot or a Shapiro-Wilk test.
- There are several variations of this test, including Bartlett's test (which is not as sensitive to whether your data are normal or not) and Levene's test (which is kind of like ANOVA but for comparing many different variances).

Research questions are of the form:

- Is the variance of [a quantitative variable] in [subjects who meet a particular condition or are members of a particular category] [*greater than, less than, different*] than the variance of [a quantitative variable] in [subjects who meet a particular condition or are members of a particular category]?
- Has the variance of a particular physical value *changed* since a process improvement effort was implemented?

		What it means
H₀:	$\sigma_1^2 = \sigma_2^2$	There is no difference between the population variance in the first group and the second group
Hₐ:	$\sigma_1^2 > \sigma_2^2$ (one-tailed)	One of the population variances is larger than the other

Because this is an F-test, the Test Statistic (T.S.) that you will calculate will be a **F**.

One sample t-test: Weight of M&M bags

In Spring 2017, my students (once again) collected data about M&Ms. **Does the weight of the full bags exceed what's printed on the bags (1.69 oz = 47.91 g)?**

```
> mnms <-
read.csv("https://docs.google.com/spreadsheets/d/1p3L6w6L1ZxIT7lJtN5CJmu2niPlHUfkQEvgC
1wBqn3E/pub?gid=0&single=true&output=csv")
> head(mnms)
  student id color defect full.bag.weight empty.bag.weight total.number
1  alborb  1     R     N        49.36            1.02              55
2  alborb  2    BR     L        49.36            1.02              55
3  alborb  3     G     N        49.36            1.02              55
4  alborb  4     R     C        49.36            1.02              55
5  alborb  5     R     N        49.36            1.02              55
6  alborb  6    BL     N        49.36            1.02              55
```

Even though each observation (row) corresponds to one M&M candy, we logged the bag weight (which corresponds to many M&Ms) once per row. This isn't the best way to record data, but we have to work with it. First, let's use the aggregate command to collapse each student's 50 or so observations into one row per student. This allows us to shift our level of analysis from the individual M&Ms to the bags. Notice that you can't realistically determine a student's *average color of M&Ms* or *average defect* per bag, since they are categorical variables, so the "average values" reported will just be NA (for "not available").

```
> agg.mnms <- aggregate(mnms, by=list(mnms$student), FUN=mean, na.rm=TRUE)
There were 50 or more warnings (use warnings() to see the first 50)
> head(agg.mnms)
  Group.1  student    id color defect full.bag.weight empty.bag.weight total.number
1  alborb   NA 28.0    NA    NA        49.36            1.02              55
2  ALQASAA  NA 28.0    NA    NA        49.15            1.05              55
3  bretziwa NA 27.5    NA    NA        48.70            1.02              54
4  chamb2mj NA 28.5    NA    NA        49.09            1.05              56
5  collieec NA 28.0    NA    NA        48.17            1.01              55
6  craigce  NA 29.0    NA    NA        51.19            0.99              57
```

Next, let's gather the information that we'll need to calculate the test statistic, and check out a histogram of the bag weights as well:

```
> mean(agg.mnms$full.bag.weight)
[1] 48.90875
> sd(agg.mnms$full.bag.weight)
[1] 1.299332
> length(agg.mnms$full.bag.weight)
[1] 24
> hist(agg.mnms$full.bag.weight, col="lightpurple", breaks=8)
```

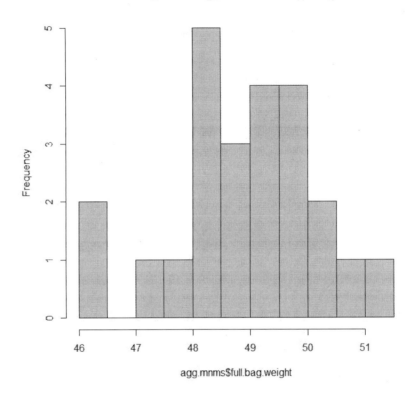

Histogram of agg.mnms$full.bag.weight

Step 0: Check Assumptions
- **Random sample** - We can assume that we purchased a random sample of M&Ms from the universe of potential bags of M&Ms. ✔
- **Observations are independent** - It is unlikely that the characteristics of one bag of M&Ms will affect the characteristics of another bag. ✔
- **Sample is small enough** - Is our sample of n=24 bags less than 10% of the size of the entire population of bags of M&Ms? Absolutely. ✔
- **Sample is large enough, or distributions are nearly normal** - The histogram for all 24 bags is approximately bell shaped, and the sample is not tiny. ✔

Step 1: Set Null (H₀) & Alternative (Hₐ) Hypotheses:

H₀: $\mu = \mu_0$ μ_0 is the standard, target, or recommended value. Set $\mu_0 = 47.91$ g

Hₐ: $\mu > \mu_0$ ... and then you PICK ONE from the alternatives. Based on our
        $\mu < \mu_0$ histogram, let's check and see if our bags are *heavier* than
        $\mu \neq \mu_0$ advertised.

Step 2: Set α, the Level of Significance:

An **α of 0.05** means that **1 out of every 20 times** we collect data to run this test, we accept that we will *reject the null hypothesis* when that's the wrong answer. Is this OK? There are three things we have to consider: **cost** of getting new data, the **risk** of making an incorrect decision based on this test, and the **ethical considerations** associated with someone else using our results to make *their* decisions.

- **First**, does it cost a lot to get more data? Not really. Each bag costs about a dollar.
- **Second**, what decision will I make based on this test? None. I'm just curious. If I worked for the M&M company, I might be making a decision to change the weight I print on my labels, which is a pretty big decision... in which case I might want to choose a more stringent alpha.
- **Finally**, will anyone else be using my data or analysis to make *their* decisions? No. This is just for my own curiosity.

As a result, it's perfectly reasonable to use **0.05** as our level of significance.

Step 3: Calculate Test Statistic (T.S.)

This is a one sample t-test, so the test statistic we want to compute is a **t.** (This also means we will use the t distribution, which is almost identical to the bell-shaped normal distribution). We know the mean weight, the target we're comparing our data to, and the standard deviations of the weights, so we just plug the values in:

$$t = \frac{\overline{y} - \mu_0}{SE(\overline{y})} = \frac{\overline{y} - \mu_0}{s/\sqrt{n}}$$

1   One-Sample t-test (Weight)

$$t = \frac{\bar{y} - \mu_0}{SE(\bar{y})} = \frac{48.91 - 47.91}{1.30/\sqrt{24}} = 3.77$$

Step 4: Draw a Picture

The value of t that we calculated is approximately t=+3.77. This is far to the right of the mean in the distribution that we're using to represent our null hypothesis. By making an arrow out of the sign in our alternative hypothesis, we know to shade the area to the right of t=+3.77. The picture shows the area we will be trying to find in Step 5, which is nearly 0% if we consider the 68-95-99.7 rule.

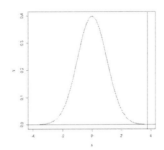

Here's the code that produced this plot (it's not even shaded because the area in the tail is so tiny).

```
x <- seq(-4,4,0.1)
y <- dnorm(x)
plot(x,y,type="l")
abline(h=0)
abline(v=+3.77)
```

Step 5: Calculate P-Value

From Step 4, we estimated that the total area (our P-value) will be approximately 0%. Now let's find out exactly how large the shaded area is. Due to symmetry, the area of the tail left of t=-3.77 is the same as the area in the tail to the right of t=+3.77. We will look up the left area:

```
> pt(-3.77,df=24)
[1] 0.0004701051
```

Because our sample size is large enough, we could have used the normal distribution as an approximation to the t distribution to look up this area. There's no appreciable difference between areas that are this tiny.

```
> pnorm(-3.77)
[1] 8.162377e-05
```

Step 6: Draw Conclusion

Is the P-Value < α? If so, reject the null hypothesis (H$_0$).

Is (almost zero) < 0.05? **Yes.** We **reject** the null hypothesis (H$_0$) that the weight of our bags in 47.91 g. **It seems that our bags are indeed heavier than advertised.**

(**Note:** You can stop here if you like. The remaining steps provide additional information that usually corroborates the conclusion you just drew.)

Step 7: Compute Confidence Interval & Double Check in R

We can double check this conclusion by computing the confidence interval - that is, using the data we have to cast a net around. All confidence intervals are of the form:

$$CI: \quad Estimate \pm Margin\ of\ Error\ (ME)$$

For the case of one mean, our estimate is just the mean value of our quantitative variable. The margin of error depends on two things: how big a net we *want* (a 90%, or 95%, or 99% confidence interval) and how big a net we *need* (for smaller samples, we can't be as certain of the variability in the population, so we'll need a bigger net).

$$CI: \quad Estimate \pm (How\ Big\ a\ Net\ we\ Want)\ x\ (How\ Big\ a\ Net\ we\ Need)$$

$$CI: \quad Estimate \pm t_{df}^* \ x\ Standard\ Error\ of\ the\ Mean$$

We look up t_{df}^* based on how confident we want to be that we've captured the true mean weight of the bags, and we plug in values from our collected data to calculate the rest. For a 95% confidence interval, we get the critical t value t_{df}^* using the qt command in R, being sure to specify the degrees of freedom (which will be one less than the number of observations in our bag of data).

```
> qt(0.975,df=23)
[1] 2.068658
```

If we want a 95% confidence interval, we have to give the qt command a 0.975 value, because the qt command only looks up t values when you give it the *entire area* to the left of that t value, while confidence intervals have *two* tails you have to account for. (If this is confusing, just memorize that you need to give qt 0.95 for a 90% confidence interval, 0.975 to get a 95% confidence interval, and 0.995 for a 99% confidence interval. This is the percent confidence interval you want, *plus the left tail*.) Now we can plug in all the values and find the confidence interval:

$$\bar{y} \pm t^*_{df} \frac{s}{\sqrt{n}}$$

$$48.9 \pm 2.07x \frac{1.3}{\sqrt{24}} = 48.9 \pm 0.55$$

By subtracting 0.55 from the weight estimate of 48.9, we get a lower bound of 48.35 g. By adding 0.55, we get an upper bound of 49.45 g. **We are 95% confident that the true weight of the bags is between 48.35 g and 49.45 g.** (Always interpret your confidence interval by saying, or writing, *this entire sentence.*)

Notice how the standard, target, or recommended value that we compared our data to (47.91 g) isn't *anywhere near* the inside of this confidence interval? It's not a possible weight, according to our tests. This corroborates the result of our inference test: we *rejected* the null hypothesis that the true weight was 47.91 g. And here, in our confidence interval, we see again that out of the possible values we've identified for the bag weight -- that is, everything between the lower and upper bounds of our CI -- 47.91 g is just not there.

Let's see how R answers our research question:

```
> t.test(agg.mnms$full.bag.weight,mu=47.91,alternative="greater")

        One Sample t-test

data:  agg.mnms$full.bag.weight
t = 3.7657, df = 23, p-value = 0.0005024
alternative hypothesis: true mean is greater than 47.91
95 percent confidence interval:
48.45419      Inf
sample estimates:
```

```
mean of x
48.90875
```

Notice that the test statistic t (3.7657) is exactly what we calculated (3.77), and we also find a p-value that's very close to zero, indicating that we should reject our null hypothesis that the average bag weight is 47.91 g. Unfortunately, the confidence interval looks a little funky... positive infinity (Inf) can't be an upper bound! To solve this problem, we just remove the `alternative="greater"` argument from t.test and run again:

```
> t.test(agg.mnms$full.bag.weight,mu=47.91)

        One Sample t-test

data:  agg.mnms$full.bag.weight
t = 3.7657, df = 23, p-value = 0.001005
alternative hypothesis: true mean is not equal to 47.91
95 percent confidence interval:
 48.36009 49.45741
sample estimates:
mean of x
 48.90875
```

We are 95% confident that the true weight of the bags is between 48.36 g and 49.46 g. This is *almost exactly* what we got when we computed the limits of the confidence interval analytically.

Appendix

[Note: Realistically, our bags *aren't* heavier than advertised. We also have `empty.bag.weight` in our data, and if you do a paired t-test to see if the difference between full and empty bag weights is *different* than 47.91 g, you see that it's not. What this means is that the published value of 47.91 g is *only* for the M&Ms, and does not include the weight of the empty bag.]

```
> t.test(agg.mnms$full.bag.weight,agg.mnms$empty.bag.weight,mu=47.91,paired=TRUE)

        Paired t-test

data:  agg.mnms$full.bag.weight and agg.mnms$empty.bag.weight
t = -0.048848, df = 23, p-value = 0.9615
alternative hypothesis: true difference in means is not equal to 47.91
95 percent confidence interval:
 47.35008 48.44409
sample estimates:
mean of the differences
               47.89708
```

One sample t-test: Diameter of PVC Pipe

We produce 6" lengths of PVC pipe with a diameter of 1.3" using an extrusion process. In addition to control charting to make sure our production process stays in control, we also check to make sure that (on average) the physical parameters are meeting our specifications. Using a random sample of the PVC pipes we produce on a daily basis, we want to know: **Are we meeting our specification for producing PVC pipe with a diameter of 1.3"?**

```
pvc <-
c(1.301,1.299,1.287,1.302,1.303,1.300,1.297,1.296,1.301,1.299,1.298,1.304,1.302,1.297,
1.298,1.299,1.299,1.297,1.304,1.303,1.301,1.300,1.298,1.299,1.296,1.302,1.298,1.302,1.
300,1.303,1.299,1.297,1.296,1.304,1.300,1.301,1.299,1.297,1.298,1.301,1.301,1.299)
```

First, let's gather the information that we'll need to calculate the test statistic, and check out a histogram of the PVC diameters as well:

```
> mean(pvc)
[1] 1.299452
> sd(pvc)
[1] 0.003021891
> length(pvc)
[1] 42
> hist(pvc,col="yellow",breaks=8)
```

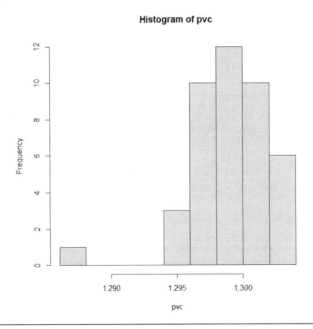

Step 0: Check Assumptions

- **Random sample** - We used systematic sampling to ensure that we collected a random sample. Every 500th pipe segment that was produced today became part of our sample. ✔
- **Observations are independent** - The measurement from one pipe does not influence the measurement from another pipe. ✔
- **Sample is small enough** - Is our sample of n=42 pipes less than 10% of the size of the entire population of pipes produced in one day? Yes, there are more than 420 pipes produced at this plant every day. In fact, we produce nearly 10000 pipes a day. ✔
- **Sample is large enough, or distributions are nearly normal** - The histogram for all 42 measurements is approximately bell shaped, and the sample is not tiny (< 30). ✔

Step 1: Set Null (H_0) & Alternative (H_a) Hypotheses:

H_0: $\mu = \mu_0$ μ_0 is the standard, target, or recommended value. Set $\mu_0 = 1.300$

H_a: $\mu > \mu_0$ ... and then PICK ONE version from the alternatives. We want to
$\mu < \mu_0$ know if our pipes measure *exactly* to our specification. Too small
$\mu \neq \mu_0$ is bad, and too large is also bad. We pick the last ($\neq$) option.

Step 2: Set α, the Level of Significance:

An **α of 0.05** means that **1 out of every 20 times** we collect data to run this test, we accept that we will *reject the null hypothesis* when that's the wrong answer. Is this OK? There are three things we have to consider: **cost** of getting new data, the **risk** of making an incorrect decision based on this test, and the **ethical considerations** associated with someone else using our results to make *their* decisions.

- First, does it cost a lot to get more data? No. This data is cheap, and easy to collect. We make pipes every day, and we could easily collect more data each day.
- Second, what decision will I make based on this test? We take our production quality seriously. If this test shows that our pipes are not (on average) meeting the specification, then we may have a problem. We'll spend time, effort, and maybe money to solve that problem. So there's a lot at stake.

- Finally, will anyone else be using my data or analysis to make *their* decisions? Yes. There are lots of people working in the PVC pipe company who might use this data to make different decisions. As a result, I need to be very careful about how I publish and share my data, analysis, and conclusions.

As a result, let's instead choose an **α of 0.01,** meaning that **1 out of every 100 times** we run this test, we will *reject the null hypothesis* when that's the wrong thing to do. If we draw this conclusion, we're going to invest time, effort, and maybe money chasing a problem that doesn't exist. But by choosing this value for our level of significance, we're establishing a basis for acceptable risk: if we draw an incorrect conclusion one time we run this test every 100, that's OK.

Step 3: Calculate Test Statistic (T.S.)

This is a one sample t-test, so the test statistic we want to compute is a **t.** (This also means we will use the t distribution, which is almost identical to the bell-shaped normal distribution). We know the mean diameter, the specification we're comparing our measurements to, and the standard deviations of the diameters, so we just plug the values in:

$$t = \frac{\bar{y} - \mu_0}{SE(\bar{y})} = \frac{\bar{y} - \mu_0}{s/\sqrt{n}}$$

$$t = \frac{\bar{y} - \mu_0}{s/\sqrt{n}} = \frac{1.299452 - 1.30}{0.003022/\sqrt{42}} = -1.175$$

Step 4: Draw a Picture

The value of t that we calculated is approximately t=-1.175. This is well to the left of the mean in the distribution that we're using to represent our null hypothesis. By making an arrow out of the sign in our alternative hypothesis, we know to shade the area to the left of t=-1.175 *and* in the opposite tail to the right of. The picture shows the area we will be trying to find in Step 5. By the 68-95-99.7 Rule, we know it will be slightly higher than 20%. Here's the code to produce this plot:

```
x <- seq(-4,4,0.1)
y <- dnorm(x)
plot(x,y,type="l")
abline(h=0)
abline(v=-1.2) # Estimate for -1.175
abline(v=+1.2) # Estimate for +1.175
```

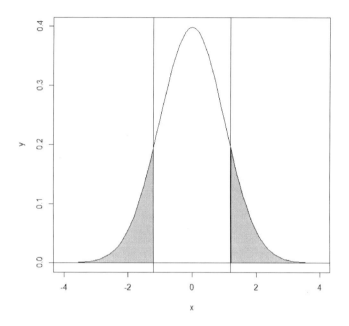

```
> # Create shaded area with polygon command
> which(x=="-1.2")
[1] 29
> which(x=="1.2")
[1] 53
> # My bounds are at x[29] and x[53]
        polygon(c(x[1:29],rev(x[1:29])), c(rep(0,29),rev(y[1:29])), col="lightgray")
        polygon(c(x[53:81],rev(x[53:81])), c(rep(0,29),rev(y[53:81])),
        col="lightgray")
```

Step 5: Calculate P-Value

From Step 4, we estimated that the total shaded area (our P-value) will be around 20%. Now let's find out *exactly* how large the shaded area is. Due to symmetry, the area of the tail left of t=-1.175 is the same as the area to the right of t=+1.175. Look up the left area and multiply by 2 for the total:

```
> 2 * pt(-1.175,df=42)
[1] 0.2466133
```

Since `df` is high, the normal distribution would probably have been sufficient to determine the area:

```
> 2 * pnorm(-1.175)
[1] 0.2399947
```

Step 6: Draw Conclusion

Is the P-Value < α? If so, reject the null hypothesis (H₀).

Is 0.24 < 0.01? **No way.** We **fail to reject** the null hypothesis (H₀) that the diameters of the PVC pipes we have produced today are different than 1.300. **We are meeting our specifications.**

Step 7: Compute Confidence Interval & Double Check in R

We start with the general form of the confidence interval, and then substitute in the equations for the one-sample t-test:

$$CI : Estimate \pm Margin\ of\ Error$$

$$\overline{y} \pm t^*_{df} SE(\overline{y})$$

From p. 38, we know that the Standard Error is 0.003022 divided by the square root of 42 (which is 0.000466). Now all we need to compute the confidence interval is the critical t, which we can look up. We need to know the secret to using `qt`, which is to feed it the size of our confidence interval *plus half of the remaining tails*. So for a 95% CI, we have to give `qt` a value of 0.975, which is 0.95 plus half of the remaining area that's in the left tail. We have to do this because R gives (and looks up) areas to the *left* of a test statistic.

```
> qt(0.975,df=41)
[1] 2.019541
```

Now we can plug all our values into the expression for confidence interval:

```
> mean(pvc) + c(-2.0195*0.000466, 2.0195*0.000466)
[1] 1.298511 1.300393
```

We are 95% confident that the true diameter of the PVC pipe is between 1.298511" and 1.300393". Our target of 1.30" is inside this confidence interval, which supports our decision to *fail to reject* the null hypothesis. We started out thinking our pipes had a diameter of 1.30", and after our data analysis, we can stick to that view of the world.

Finally, we verify our work in R:

```
> t.test(pvc,mu=1.3)

        One Sample t-test

data:  pvc
t = -1.1744, df = 41, p-value = 0.247
alternative hypothesis: true mean is not equal to 1.3
95 percent confidence interval:
 1.298511 1.300394
sample estimates:
mean of x
 1.299452
```

The test statistic, P-Value, and confidence interval are very nearly what we calculated analytically. Our work here is done.

One sample t-test: GPAs

In 2013, I found out from the University Registrar that the average Grade Point Average (GPA) of all students at our university was 3.2 on a scale of 0 to 4. This semester, I asked 36 students their cumulative GPAs. **Has the average GPA increased since 2013?**

```
gpas <- c(3.11,2.9,2.78,3.45,3.89,3.9,2.0,3.0,3.14,3.13,3.38,3.31,
3.28,3.79,3.62,3.5,3.1,3.08,3.19,2.78,2.65,3.5,3.66,3.2,2.38,4.0,3.79,3.2,3.
8,3.01,2.97,3.43,3.19,3.2,3.49,3.16)
```

First, let's gather the information that we'll need to calculate the test statistic, and check out a histogram of the GPAs as well:

```
> mean(gpas)
[1] 3.248889
> sd(gpas)
[1] 0.4284242
> hist(gpas,col="lightblue",breaks=8)
```

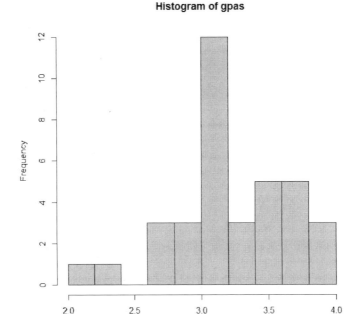

Step 0: Check Assumptions

- **Random sample** - We used multistage sampling to ensure that we collected a random and representative sample. First, five clusters were identified based on where students usually eat lunch. Within each cluster, we performed systematic sampling, and asked every 5th person in line for lunch to provide their GPA. ✔

- **Observations are independent** - We allowed respondents to write their GPA on a small slip of paper to ensure privacy. As a result, we believe our observations are independent. ✔

- **Sample is small enough** - Is our sample of n=36 students less than 10% of the size of the entire student population at our university? Yes, I definitely expect that there are more than 360 students at our school. ✔

- **Sample is large enough, or distributions are nearly normal** - The histogram for all 36 students' GPAs is approximately bell shaped, and the sample is not tiny. ✔

Step 1: Set Null (H_0) & Alternative (H_a) Hypotheses:

H_0: $\mu = \mu_0$ μ_0 is the standard, target, or recommended value. Set $\mu_0 = 3.2$

H_a: $\mu > \mu_0$ ... and then you PICK ONE version from the alternatives. We want
           $\mu < \mu_0$ to know if students are getting *higher* GPAs than 3.2 now, so we
           $\mu \neq \mu_0$ pick the *greater than* (first) option.

Step 2: Set α, the Level of Significance:

An **α of 0.05** means that **1 out of every 20 times** we collect data to run this test, we accept that we will *reject the null hypothesis* when that's the wrong answer. Is this OK? There are three things we have to consider: **cost** of getting new data, the **risk** of making an incorrect decision based on this test, and the **ethical considerations** associated with someone else using our results to make *their* decisions.

- First, does it cost a lot to get more data? No. This data is cheap, and easy to collect.
- Second, what decision will I make based on this test? Nothing. I'm just curious.
- Finally, will anyone else be using my data or analysis to make *their* decisions? No. This is just for my own curiosity.

As a result, it's perfectly reasonable to use **0.05** as our level of significance.

Step 3: Calculate Test Statistic (T.S.)

This is a one sample t-test, so the test statistic we want to compute is a **t**. (This also means we will use the t distribution, which is almost identical to the bell-shaped normal distribution). We know the mean GPA, the target we're comparing our data to, and the standard deviations of the GPAs, so we just plug the values in:

$$t = \frac{\bar{y} - \mu_0}{SE(\bar{y})} = \frac{\bar{y} - \mu_0}{s/\sqrt{n}}$$

$$t = \frac{\bar{y} - \mu_0}{SE(\bar{y})} = \frac{3.25 - 3.2}{0.43/\sqrt{36}} = 0.698$$

Step 4: Draw a Picture

The value of t that we calculated is approximately t=+0.7. This is a little to the right of the mean in the distribution that we're using to represent our null hypothesis. By making an arrow out of the sign in our alternative hypothesis, we know to shade the area to the right of t=+0.7. The picture shows the area we will be trying to find in Step 5, which is a little bit more than 16% if we consider the 68-95-99.7 rule (so maybe 20%).

Here's the code that produced this plot:

```
x <- seq(-4,4,0.1)
y <- dnorm(x)
plot(x,y,type="l")
abline(h=0)
abline(v=+0.69)

> which(x=="0.7")
[1] 48
> polygon(c(x[48:81],rev(x[48:81])), c(rep(0,34),rev(y[48:81])), col="lightgray")
```

Step 5: Calculate P-Value

From Step 4, we estimated that the total area (our P-value) will be approximately 20%. Now let's find out exactly how large the shaded area is. Due to symmetry, the area of the tail left of t=-0.7 is the same as the area in the tail to the right of t=+0.7. We will look up the left area:

```
> pt(-0.7,df=35)
[1] 0.2442772
```

Because our sample size is large enough, we could have used the normal distribution as an approximation to the t distribution to look up this area. There's no appreciable difference between areas that are this tiny.

```
> pnorm(-0.7)
[1] 0.2419637
```

Step 6: Draw Conclusion

Is the P-Value < α? If so, reject the null hypothesis (H₀).

Is 0.24 < 0.05? **No, it is not.** We **fail to reject** the null hypothesis (H₀) that the average GPA among students at our university is 3.2. **The average GPA of 3.2 is still plausible.**

Step 7: Compute Confidence Interval & Double Check in R

We start with the general form of the confidence interval, and then substitute in the equations for the one-sample t-test:

$$CI : Estimate \pm Margin\ of\ Error$$

$$\overline{y} \pm t^*_{df} SE(\overline{y})$$

This time, let's do a 99% confidence interval. First, we find the critical t (t*) for df=35. We feed `qt` the size of our confidence interval *plus half of the remaining tails* because R gives (and looks up) areas to the *left* of a test statistic. From `qt(0.995,df=35)` we get 2.724. Calculate the margin of error (ME), then subtract (and add) it to the mean of our GPAs to find the bounds of the confidence interval.

```
> ME <- 2.724 * (.43/sqrt(36))
> mean(gpas) + c(-ME, ME)
[1] 3.053669 3.444109
```

We are 99% confident that the true average GPA at our school is between 3.054 and 3.444. Finally, double check in R. The test statistic and P-Value are the same as what we calculated analytically:

```
> t.test(gpas,mu=3.2,alternative="greater")

        One Sample t-test

data:  gpas
t = 0.68468, df = 35, p-value = 0.249
alternative hypothesis: true mean is greater than 3.2
95 percent confidence interval:
3.128247       Inf
sample estimates:
mean of x
3.248889
```

Taking the `alternative="greater"` argument out, the bounds of the CI are what we expect as well:

```
> t.test(gpas,mu=3.2,conf.level=0.99)

        One Sample t-test

data:  gpas
t = 0.68468, df = 35, p-value = 0.4981
alternative hypothesis: true mean is not equal to 3.2
99 percent confidence interval:
 3.054398 3.443380
sample estimates:
mean of x
 3.248889
```

Two-sample t test (Equal Variances):
Male and Female Heights

On 2/13/2017 we gathered heights (in cm) from 16 males and 4 females. We wanted to answer the question: **Are male students taller than female students?** We took a convenience sample of 20 students in the class to find out, recording the heights in centimeters. Here's how to get the data:

```
> tests <-
read.csv("https://docs.google.com/spreadsheets/d/178wfUixaQH36HtIvAMGOGcQsgWcidHQO5I_u
UXF3V_Y/pub?gid=0&single=true&output=csv")
> head(tests)
  height gender
1 190.50      M
2 176.50      M
3 167.64      F
4 175.00      M
5 172.70      F
6 190.50      M
```

First, separate the data into two groups: guys (gender = M) and women (gender = F):

```
> m <- tests[tests$gender=="M",]$height   # isolate heights of males only
> f <- tests[tests$gender=="F",]$height   # isolate heights of females only
> mean(m); mean(f)            # these will be the values of ybar1 and ybar2
[1] 181.542
[1] 164.46
> sd(m); sd(f)                # these will be the values of s1 and s2
[1] 8.680077
[1] 6.986749
> par(mfrow=c(1,2))
> hist(m,xlim=c(150,200));hist(f,xlim=c(150,200))
```

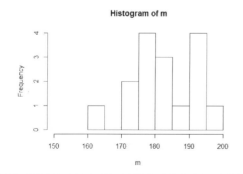
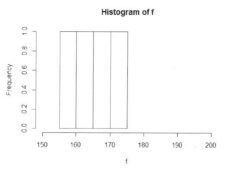

Step 0: Check Assumptions

- **Are the variances equal?** We need to know this so we know whether to use the equal variances form of this test, or the unequal variances form. First, we run var.test, and next we ask the question "Is the P-Value < about 0.05? If so, reject the null hypothesis (which says the variances are equal)." The results below show that **we should use the equal variances test**... P-Value is not tiny at all.

```
> var.test(m,f)


        F test to compare two variances

data:  m and f
F = 1.5435, num df = 15, denom df = 3, p-value = 0.8073
alternative hypothesis: true ratio of variances is not equal to 1
95 percent confidence interval:
0.1082927 6.4097089
sample estimates:
ratio of variances
         1.543465
```

- **Random sample** - It's not technically a random sample, because it's not representative of the entire student population. But we can consider that the group of students who took this exam are a random sample of all students - in all semesters - who have, or will, take this exam. ☑
- **Observations are independent** - Does one person's height influence another person's height? Definitely not. (That would be weird.) ☑
- **Sample is small enough** - Is our sample of n=20 students less than 10% of the size of the entire student population? Yes, I definitely expect that at least 200 students are enrolled at the university (in fact, there are a little over 20,000 of them). ☑
- **Sample is large enough, or distributions are nearly normal** - This assumption doesn't really check out because our samples are small, and the distribution of women's heights is uniform (it looks like a plateau or a mesa). But for the purposes of this example, we're going to go ahead with the analysis.

```
> length(m)         # this will be the value of our n1 variable
[1] 16
> length(f)         # this will be the value of our n2 variable
[1] 4
```

Step 1: Set Null (H₀) & Alternative (Hₐ) Hypotheses

H_0: $\mu_{Males} - \mu_{Females} = D_0$ D_0 is the difference you *think* exists between the means of the groups. Set $D_0 = 0$ to start with the assumption that men and women have equal heights.

H_a: $\mu_{Males} - \mu_{Females} > D_0$ We PICK ONE version from the alternatives. From
          $\mu_{Males} - \mu_{Females} < D_0$ the data, it looks like men are taller, so we pick the first
          $\mu_{Males} - \mu_{Females} \neq D_0$ (greater than) option.

Step 2: Set α, the Level of Significance

An **α of 0.05** means that **1 out of every 20 times** we collect data to run this test, we accept that we will *reject the null hypothesis* when that's the wrong answer. Is this OK? There are three things we have to consider: **cost** of getting new data, the **risk** of making an incorrect decision based on this test, and the **ethical considerations** associated with someone else using our results to make *their* decisions.

- First, does it cost a lot to get more data? The answer is **no**. It would be cheap and easy to find out the heights and genders of a few more students.
- Second, what decision will I make based on this test? This test is just for my curiosity.
- Finally, will anyone else be using my data or analysis to make *their* decisions? No. No one will be making policy decisions based on my test.

We stick with our initial alpha.

Step 3: Calculate Test Statistic (T.S.)

This is a two-sample t-test, so the test statistic we want to compute is a **t**. (This also means we will use the t distribution, which is almost identical to the bell-shaped normal distribution). We know the means from each of our two groups (y-bars), we know that D_0 is 0, we know the standard deviations from each of our two groups (s), and we know how many items are in each group (n) so this is just a matter of plugging values in:

$$t = \frac{\bar{y}_1 - \bar{y}_2 - D_0}{SE_{pooled}(\bar{y}_1 - \bar{y}_2)} = \frac{\bar{y}_1 - \bar{y}_2 - D_0}{s_p\sqrt{\frac{1}{n_1} + \frac{1}{n_2}}}$$

However, we do need to look up the formula for pooled standard deviation, s_p:

$$s_p = \sqrt{\frac{(n_1 - 1)s_1^2 + (n_2 - 1)s_2^2}{n_1 + n_2 - 2}}$$

Let's calculate s_p first:

$$s_p = \sqrt{\frac{(15)8.68^2 + (3)6.99^2}{16 + 4 - 2}} = 8.42$$

"Pooled" standard deviation should be somewhere between the standard deviation of the two groups. Indeed, 8.42 is between 8.68 and 6.99, and it's closer to the value for our males group (which had lots more members). This indicates that our s_p appears correct. Now we plug in all the values to find our test statistic t:

$$t = \frac{181.542 - 164.46}{8.42\sqrt{\frac{1}{16} + \frac{1}{3}}} = 3.629$$

Step 4: Draw a Picture

The value of t that we calculated is t=+3.63. This is far to the right of the mean of the distribution that we're using to represent our null hypothesis, and even beyond the bounds of the largest area from the 68-95-99.7 rule. As a result, we know that the area of the right tail beyond t=+3.63 (the P-Value) will be *significantly* less than 1%, and we don't need to draw a picture.

Step 5: Calculate P-Value

From Step 4, we estimated that the total area (our P-value) will be < 1%. Now let's find out exactly how large the shaded area is:

```
> 1 - pt(3.63,df=16+4-2)
[1] 0.0009575054
```

Our sample size is pretty small, so we could not have used the normal distribution (pnorm) to estimate the P-Value. There will be a substantial difference between the t distribution and the normal distribution for this particular model.

Step 6: Draw Conclusion & Compute CI

Is the P-Value < α? If so, reject the null hypothesis (H₀).

Is 0.00096 < 0.05? **Yes, for sure.** We **reject** the null hypothesis (H₀) that there is no difference between the heights of the guys and the heights of the women. We have evidence that suggests **guys are taller than women.**

Step 7: Compute Confidence Interval & Double Check in R

First, recall that the standard error of the difference that we calculated earlier was 4.71 - the denominator from our calculation of the test statistic t earlier. (We'll use that value shortly). Next, let's create a 95% confidence interval. First, start with the general form of the CI:

CI: Estimate ± Margin of Error

)

Estimate ± (t$_{df}$* x Standard Error of the Estimate)

$$(\bar{y}_1 - \bar{y}_2) \pm t^*_{df} SE(\bar{y}_1 - \bar{y}_2)$$

We know the Estimate (that's the difference between the mean male height and the mean female height), we can look up the t* for a 95% CI with 18 degrees of freedom, and we can use the standard error we calculated earlier when we were figuring out the test statistic. So, just plug in those numbers to get the lower and upper bounds of the CI:

```
> ME <- qt(0.975,df=18) * 4.71
> (181.542-164.40) + c(-ME,+ME)
[1]   7.246657 27.037343
```

We are 95% confident that male students are between 7.25 and 27.04 cm taller than females.

That means we are 95% confident that the true difference in heights is *at least 7.25 cm.* Guys are a LOT taller! No wonder we rejected the null hypothesis... **a difference of zero (which is what we were testing for) is far, far outside the lower bound of this interval.** Let's run it in R to check:

```
> t.test(m,f,alternative="greater",var.equal=TRUE)

        Two Sample t-test

data:  m and f
t = 3.6285, df = 18, p-value = 0.0009608
alternative hypothesis: true difference in means is greater than 0
95 percent confidence interval:
 8.918409        Inf
sample estimates:
mean of x mean of y
  181.542   164.460
```

All of the values are very close to what we calculated analytically, except the confidence interval. We need to drop the alternative to compute CI correctly:

```
> t.test(m,f,var.equal=TRUE)

        Two Sample t-test

data:  m and f
t = 3.6285, df = 18, p-value = 0.001922
alternative hypothesis: true difference in means is not equal to 0
95 percent confidence interval:
  7.19132 26.97268
sample estimates:
mean of x mean of y
  181.542   164.460
```

Yes, the males are taller than the females, a conclusion that is also supported by the boxplot:

```
> boxplot(m,f,names=c("Males","Females"))
```

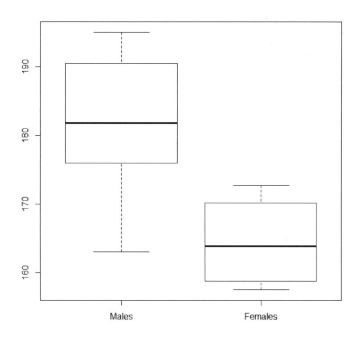

Two-sample t test (Equal Variances): Exam Scores

In Fall 2016, 52 students took my first test in my introductory statistics and data science class. I thought that the students who completed optional formula worksheets prior to the exam scored better than the ones who did not. After the second exam, I wanted to know: **Is there a difference in Exam 2 scores between people who completed the worksheets, and people who did not?**

```
> scores <-
read.csv("https://docs.google.com/spreadsheets/d/1lyqbeRdZayUrZrXD7X0__tx5WrXgNlbE9S10
61BNS6o/pub?gid=0&single=true&output=csv",header=TRUE)
> head(scores)
  student     exam1 pass worksheets num.wkshts exam2
1       1        88   Y          Y           6    85
2       2        90   Y          Y           5    90
3       3        57   N          N           0    91
4       4        70   N          N           0    77
5       5        72   N          N           0    82
6       6        87   Y          Y           3    89
```

Before we get started, separate the data into two groups (`worksheets=Y` and `worksheets=N`) and to generate descriptive statistics:

```
> yes <- scores[scores$worksheets=="Y",]$exam2    # scores from will be GROUP 1
> no <- scores[scores$worksheets=="N",]$exam2     # this will be GROUP 2
> mean(yes); mean(no)           # these will be the values of ybar1 and ybar2
[1] 87.57143
[1] 88.6129
> sd(yes); sd(no)                     # these will be the values of s1 and s2
[1] 4.975655
[1] 5.565833
> par(mfrow=c(1,2))
> hist(yes,xlim=c(0,100));hist(no,xlim=c(0,100))
```

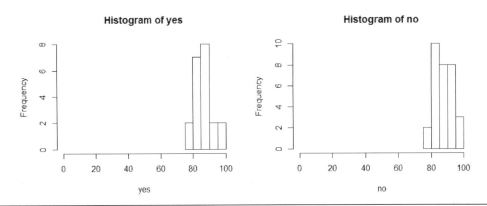

Step 0: Check Assumptions

- **Are the variances within the two groups the same, or different?** By looking at the histograms for the two groups, it looks like the variance in the "yes" group is much smaller than in the "no" group. To test this, we run a two-sample variance test in R. Since the P-value (0.6089) was large, we fail to reject the null hypothesis that the two groups have equal variance and use the **Two-Sample t-test for Equal Variances.** ☑

```
> var.test(yes,no)

        F test to compare two variances

data:  yes and no
F = 0.79917, num df = 20, denom df = 30, p-value = 0.6089
alternative hypothesis: true ratio of variances is not equal to 1
95 percent confidence interval:
0.3640608 1.8769371
sample estimates:
ratio of variances
        0.7991719
```

- **Random sample** - It's not technically a random sample, because we have a score for each person in the class. But we can consider that the group of students who took this exam are a random sample of all students - in all semesters - who have, or will, take this exam. ☑
- **Observations are independent** - Does one person's exam score influence another person's exam score? Hopefully not. (That would probably be cheating.) ☑
- **Sample is small enough** - Is our sample of n=52 students less that 10% of the size of the entire population? Yes, I definitely expect that at least 520 students will be taking this exam at some time. ☑
- **Sample is large enough, or distributions are nearly normal** - The histograms are approximately bell shaped, and the sizes of our samples are n=21 for the "yes" group, and n=31 for the "no" group. We get this using the length command, which tells us how many items are in each bag of data.

```
> length(yes)       # this will be the value of our n1 variable
[1] 21
> length(no)        # this will be the value of our n2 variable
[1] 31
```

Step 1: Set Null (H₀) & Alternative (Hₐ) Hypotheses:

H_0: $\mu_1 - \mu_2 = D_0$ D_0 is the difference you *think* exists between the means of the two groups. We will set $D_0 = 0$ to represent the case that there has been no improvement between Exam 1 and Exam 2.

H_a: $\mu_1 - \mu_2 > D_0$ Then, we PICK ONE version from the alternatives. From the data,
         $\mu_1 - \mu_2 < D_0$ especially the histograms, **we can't tell which exam has a**
         $\mu_1 - \mu_2 \neq D_0$ higher mean, so we pick the *third* option (not equal to) for our
                        alternative hypothesis.

Step 2: Set α, the Level of Significance:

An **α of 0.05** means that **1 out of every 20 times** we collect data to run this test, we accept that we will *reject the null hypothesis* when that's the wrong answer. Is this OK? There are three things we have to consider: cost of getting new data, risk of making an incorrect decision based on this test, and the ethical considerations associated with someone else using our results to make *their* decisions.

- First, does it cost a lot to get more data? The answer is **yes**. To get a new exam score, a student has to (hopefully) study for the test, and then spend at least an hour completing the test. It's not like a survey or questionnaire where I can ask for 5 minutes of someone's time.
- Second, what decision will I make based on this test? If the scores between the two groups are about the same, then I will know that forcing the students to do 6-8 more hours of work prior to the exam was worth it - and I'll keep asking future students to make that investment. So the risk of making an incorrect decision is pretty significant for those future students.
- Finally, will anyone else be using my data or analysis to make *their* decisions? No. This is just for my personal use as an instructor... no one will be making policy decisions based on the results of my test.

I might want to consider setting α to **0.01,** meaning that I'll make the wrong decision only **1 out of every 100 times** I potentially collect data. That seems more reasonable to me for this test. There's a lot on the line... for the workloads and stress levels of my future students.

Step 3: Calculate Test Statistic (T.S.)

This is a two-sample t-test, so the test statistic we want to compute is a **t**. (This also means we will use the t distribution, which is almost identical to the bell-shaped normal distribution). We know the means from each of our two groups (y-bars), we know that D_0 is 0, we know the standard deviations from each of our two groups (s), and we know how many items are in each group (n) so this is just a matter of plugging values in:

$$t = \frac{\bar{y}_1 - \bar{y}_2 - D_0}{SE_{pooled}(\bar{y}_1 - \bar{y}_2)} = \frac{\bar{y}_1 - \bar{y}_2 - D_0}{s_p \sqrt{\frac{1}{n_1} + \frac{1}{n_2}}}$$

However, we do need to look up the formula for pooled standard deviation, s_p:

$$s_p = \sqrt{\frac{(n_1 - 1)s_1^2 + (n_2 - 1)s_2^2}{n_1 + n_2 - 2}}$$

Let's calculate s_p first:

$$s_p = \sqrt{\frac{(20)4.98^2 + (30)5.57^2}{21 + 31 - 2}} = 5.34$$

"Pooled" standard deviation should be somewhere between the standard deviation of the two groups. Indeed, 5.34 is between 4.98 and 5.57, indicating that our calculation of s_p appears to be correct. Now we can plug in all the values to find our test statistic t:

$$t = \frac{\bar{y}_1 - \bar{y}_2 - 0}{SE_{pooled}(\bar{y}_1 - \bar{y}_2)} = \frac{87.571 - 88.613}{5.34\sqrt{\frac{1}{21} + \frac{1}{31}}} = -0.69$$

Step 4: Draw a Picture

The value of t that we calculated is t=-0.69. This is just slightly to the left of the mean of the distribution that we're using to represent our null hypothesis. Since we're doing a two-tailed test (that is, we chose the H_a with the ≠ sign in it) we shade the tail to the left of t=-0.69, *and* we shade the tail to the right of t=+0.33. Using the 68-95-99.7 Rule, the area we will be trying to find in Step 5 is over 32% (the area beyond t=-1 and t=+1, or 100%-68%).

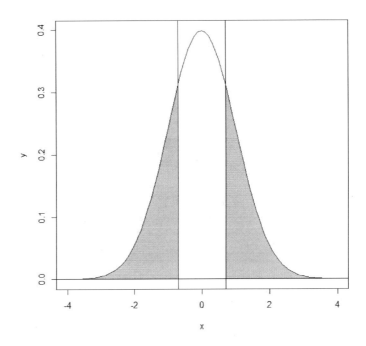

Here's the code that produced this shaded plot:

```
x <- seq(-4,4,0.1)
y <- dnorm(x)
plot(x,y,type="l")
abline(h=0)
abline(v=-0.7)
abline(v=+0.7)
```

```
> which(x=="-0.7")
[1] 34
> which(x=="0.7")
[1] 48
> polygon(c(x[1:34],rev(x[1:34])), c(rep(0,34),rev(y[1:34])), col="lightgray")
> length(x)
[1] 81
> polygon(c(x[48:81],rev(x[48:81])), c(rep(0,34),rev(y[48:81])), col="lightgray")
```

Step 5: Calculate P-Value

From Step 4, we estimated that the total area (our P-value) will be approximately 80%. Now let's find out exactly how large the shaded area is:

```
> 2 * pt(-0.69,df=21+31-2)
[1] 0.4933846
```

Because our sample size is large enough, we could have also used the normal distribution as an approximation to the t distribution, like this:

```
> 2 * pnorm(-0.69)
[1] 0.4901942
```

Step 6: Draw Conclusion

Is the P-Value < α? If so, reject the null hypothesis (H$_0$).

Is 0.49 < 0.01? **No, it is not.** We **fail to reject** the null hypothesis (H$_0$) that there is no difference between the mean exam score for students who completed the worksheets and those who did not. Surprisingly, there is no difference in exam performance. **I should not make the formula worksheets compulsory, because it looks like they are not related to exam performance.**

Step 7: Compute Confidence Interval & Double Check in R

First, recall that the Standard Error of the Difference that we calculated earlier (the denominator in our test statistic t) was 1.509. (We'll use that value shortly). Next, let's create a 95% confidence interval. First, start with the general form of the CI:

CI: Estimate ± Margin of Error

Estimate ± (t$_{df}$* x Standard Error of the Estimate)

$$(\overline{y}_1 - \overline{y}_2) \pm t_{df}^* SE(\overline{y}_1 - \overline{y}_2)$$

For a 95% confidence interval, the critical t (t*) will be `qt(0.975,df=21+31-2)` or 2.009. Now we can plug in all our values to find the confidence interval:

```
> ME <- 2.009*1.509
> (mean(yes)-mean(no)) + c(-ME,ME)
[1] -4.073056  1.990106
```

We are 95% confident that the true difference in exam scores is between -4.07 and +1.98 points. This is not that good, because it means that *zero* is a totally reasonable difference. Notice also that this supports our conclusion in Step 6 – we failed to reject the null hypothesis that the difference between test scores could be zero. Let's double check our calculations in R. Indeed, the test statistic, P-Value, and confidence interval match what we determined analytically:

```
> t.test(yes,no,var.equal=TRUE)

        Two Sample t-test

data:  yes and no
t = -0.69039, df = 50, p-value = 0.4931
alternative hypothesis: true difference in means is not equal to 0
95 percent confidence interval:
 -4.071468  1.988519
sample estimates:
mean of x mean of y
 87.57143  88.61290
```

The `boxplot(yes,no)` also corroborates the story: there is not much of a difference between these two groups of exam scores:

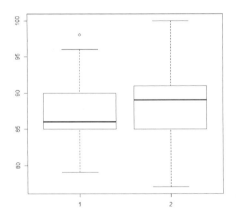

Two-sample t test (Unequal Variances): Exam Scores

In Fall 2016, 52 students took the first test in my intro class. I thought the students who completed optional worksheets prior to the exam scored better than the ones who did not. For the second exam, I wanted to see: **Is there a difference in exam scores between people who completed the worksheets, and people who did not?** I was surprised to find out that there wasn't, so I went back to Exam 1 to see if I was just imagining a difference. I performed the same test on Exam 1 scores.

```
> scores <-
read.csv("https://docs.google.com/spreadsheets/d/1lyqbeRdZayUrZrXD7X0__tx5WrXgNlbE9S10
61BNS6o/pub?gid=0&single=true&output=csv",header=TRUE)
> head(scores)
  student      exam1  pass worksheets num.wkshts exam2
1       1         88  Y            Y           6    85
2       2         90  Y            Y           5    90
3       3         57  N            N           0    91
4       4         70  N            N           0    77
5       5         72  N            N           0    82
6       6         87  Y            Y           3    89
```

Before we get started, let's separate the data into two groups (or "bags") and generate descriptive statistics. One bag will contain scores for the students who did worksheets (`worksheets=Y`) and the other will contain scores for the students who did not do worksheets (`worksheets=N`).

```
> yes <- scores[scores$worksheets=="Y",]$exam1   # scores for GROUP 1
> no <- scores[scores$worksheets=="N",]$exam1       # scores for GROUP 2
> mean(yes); mean(no)         # these will be the values of ybar1 and ybar2
[1] 91.09524
[1] 76.09677
> sd(yes); sd(no)                   # these will be the values of s1 and s2
[1] 5.393559
[1] 10.37418
> par(mfrow=c(1,2))
> hist(yes,xlim=c(0,100));hist(no,xlim=c(0,100)) # shown on next page
```

Step 0: Check Assumptions

- **Are the variances within the two groups the same, or different?** By looking at the histograms for the two groups, it looks like the variance in the "yes" group is much smaller than in the "no" group. To test this, we run a two-sample variance test in R. Since the P-value (0.003406) is tiny, we reject the null hypothesis that the two groups have equal variance and use the **Two-Sample t-test for Unequal Variances**. ✓

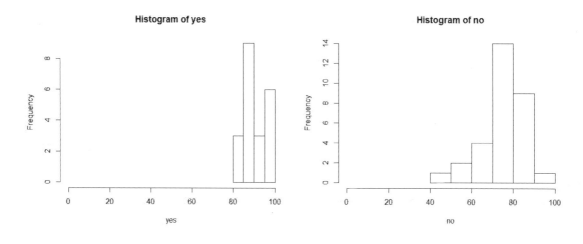

```
> var.test(yes,no)

        F test to compare two variances

data:  yes and no
F = 0.2703, num df = 20, denom df = 30, p-value = 0.003406
alternative hypothesis: true ratio of variances is not equal to 1
95 percent confidence interval:
 0.1231337 0.6348229
sample estimates:
ratio of variances
         0.2702982
```

- **Random sample** - It's not technically a random sample, because we have a score for each person in the class. But we can consider that the group of students who took this exam are a random sample of all students - in all semesters - who have, or will, take this exam. ✓
- **Observations are independent** - Does one person's exam score influence another person's exam score? Hopefully not. (That would probably be cheating.) ✓
- **Sample is small enough** - Is our sample of n=52 students less that 10% of the size of the entire population? Yes, I definitely expect that at least 520 students will be taking this exam at some time. ✓

- **Sample is large enough, or distributions are nearly normal** - The histograms are approximately bell shaped, and the sizes of our samples are n=21 for the "yes" group, and n=31 for the "no" group (almost big enough). We get this using the length command, which tells us how many items are in each bag of data.

```
> length(yes)           # this will be the value of our n1 variable
[1] 21
> length(no)            # this will be the value of our n2 variable
[1] 31
```

Step 1: Set Null (H₀) & Alternative (Hₐ) Hypotheses:

H₀:	$\mu_1 - \mu_2 = D_0$	D_0 is the difference you *think* exists between the means of the Groups. We will pick $D_0 = 0$ for *no difference between scores.*
Hₐ:	$\mu_1 - \mu_2 > D_0$ $\mu_1 - \mu_2 < D_0$ $\mu_1 - \mu_2 \neq D_0$	Next, PICK ONE version from the alternatives. From the data, it looks like the "yes" group (#1) has a higher mean score, so let's pick the first ("greater than") option for our alternative.

Step 2: Set α, the Level of Significance:

An **α of 0.05** means that **1 out of every 20 times** we collect data to run this test, we accept that we will *reject the null hypothesis* when that's the wrong answer. Is this OK? There are three things we have to consider: cost of getting new data, the risk of making an incorrect decision based on this test, and the ethical considerations associated with someone else using our results to make *their* decisions.

- First, does it cost a lot to get more data? The answer is **yes**. To get a new exam score, a student has to (hopefully) study for the test, and then spend at least an hour completing the test. It's not like a survey or questionnaire where I can ask for 5 minutes of someone's time.
- Second, what decision will I make based on this test? The answer is: if I find out that the worksheets help students perform better on the exam, then I'm going to make those worksheets mandatory in future semesters. It takes an hour or two to complete one worksheet, and you need to complete 4 or 5 worksheets to be prepared for your exam. So if I find out, by performing this test, that there's a benefit associated with completing these worksheets, I'm going to require future students to do about 8 more hours of work. That's a pretty big deal! So the risk of making an incorrect decision is pretty significant.

- Finally, will anyone else be using my data or analysis to make *their* decisions? No. This is just for my personal use as an instructor… no one will be making policy decisions based on my test.

I might want to consider setting **α** to **0.01,** meaning that I'll make the wrong decision only **1 out of every 100 times** I potentially collect data. That seems more reasonable to me for this test. There's a lot on the line… for the workloads and stress levels of my future students.

Step 3: Calculate Test Statistic (T.S.)

This is a two-sample t-test, so the test statistic we want to compute is a **t.** (This also means we will use the t distribution, which is almost identical to the bell-shaped normal distribution). We know the means from each of our two groups (y-bars), we know that D_0 is 0, we know the standard deviations from each of our two groups (s), and we know how many items are in each group (n) so this is just a matter of plugging values in:

$$t = \frac{\bar{y}_1 - \bar{y}_2 - D_0}{SE(\bar{y}_1 - \bar{y}_2)} = \frac{\bar{y}_1 - \bar{y}_2 - D_0}{\sqrt{\frac{s_1^2}{n_1} + \frac{s_2^2}{n_2}}}$$

When I plug in the values from our data, I'm going to use only one decimal place. (Why? Because when have you ever seen exam scores reported to two or three decimal places? Sometimes 2 might be OK, but never 3 for this particular variable.)

$$t = \frac{91.1 - 76.1 - D_0}{SE(\bar{y}_1 - \bar{y}_2)} = \frac{91.1 - 76.1}{\sqrt{\frac{5.4^2}{21} + \frac{10.4^2}{31}}} = 6.8$$

Step 4: Draw a Picture

The value of t that we calculated is t=+6.8. This is very, very, very far to the right of the mean of the distribution that we're using to represent our null hypothesis. By looking at the alternative hypothesis we selected, we see that we should shade to the right of t=+6.8. We don't even need to draw a picture, because the area of this tiny, tiny tail on the right side of our bell-shaped t distribution is going to be **just about zero.**

Step 5: Calculate P-Value

Our p-value, which is the area of the shaded part from our picture, will be nearly zero in this case. We don't even need to calculate an exact value, because we can report it as **p < 0.001**.

For the case of unequal variances, the degrees of freedom must be calculated using the Welch-Satterthwaite equation (on the bottom of p. 338). You can *approximate* the degrees of freedom by subtracting 2 from the total number of items across both groups (so in this case, df = 21 + 31 - 2 = 50) although the calculated version will be slightly lower than this. Regardless, the exact p-value will be extremely tiny, and with a sample size this large, the normal distribution can be used as an approximation to get the p-value:

```
> 1-pt(6.8,df=50)
[1] 6.168257e-09

> 1-pnorm(6.8)
[1] 5.230927e-12
```

Step 6: Draw Conclusion

Is the P-Value < α? If so, reject the null hypothesis (H₀).

Is (Almost Zero) < 0.01? **Yes, it is.** We reject the null hypothesis (H₀) that there is no difference between the mean exam score for students who completed the worksheets and those who did not, in favor of the alternative that students who *did* the worksheets scored better than those who did not. **Doing the worksheets appears to make a difference in exam scores!**

Step 7: Compute Confidence Interval & Double Check in R

We can examine the confidence interval as well:

CI: Estimate ± Margin of Error

$$(\bar{y}_1 - \bar{y}_2) \pm t^*_{df} \sqrt{\frac{s_1^2}{n_1} + \frac{s_2^2}{n_2}}$$

Look up the value for the critical t for a 95% confidence interval using the R command `qt(0.975,df=50)` which yields 2.01. (For a 90% CI, use 0.95, and for a 99% CI, use 0.995.) Finally, plug in the remaining values:

$$(91.1 - 76.1) \pm 2.01\sqrt{\frac{5.4^2}{21} + \frac{10.4^2}{31}}$$

$$15 \pm (2.01 \text{ x } 2.21)$$

By subtracting the margin of error from 15, we get the lower bound of 10.56, and by adding the margin of error to 15, we get the upper bound of 19.44. As a result, **we are 95% confident that the true difference in exam scores is between 10.56 and 19.44 points**. Students who completed the worksheets get, on average, anywhere between 10.56 and 19.44 more points than the students who don't complete them! **This is a pretty big difference.**

Also notice how the value zero is *not* within that confidence interval? That means zero is *not* one of the plausible values for how much of an exam score improvement we might expect to see. Because zero is the value we're using as a comparison on the right-hand side of the null hypothesis, and zero is *not* a possible value for the difference between population parameters, we know that we will reject that null hypothesis.

Checking our work in R shows the same values:

```
> t.test(yes,no,alternative="greater",var.equal=FALSE)

        Welch Two Sample t-test

data:  yes and no
t = 6.8055, df = 47.398, p-value = 7.75e-09
alternative hypothesis: true difference in means is greater than 0
95 percent confidence interval:
11.30117       Inf
sample estimates:
mean of x mean of y
91.09524   76.09677
```

And we can check the confidence interval computation by dropping the `alternative="greater"` part of the command:

```
> t.test(yes,no,var.equal=FALSE)

        Welch Two Sample t-test

data:  yes and no
t = 6.8055, df = 47.398, p-value = 1.55e-08
alternative hypothesis: true difference in means is not equal to 0
95 percent confidence interval:
10.56585 19.43107
sample estimates:
mean of x mean of y
91.09524  76.09677

> boxplot(yes,no)
```

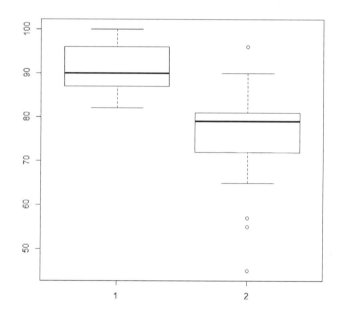

Everything checks out, and we conclude that there *is a difference* between the two groups – the students who completed the formula sheets had higher scores. What this tells me is that *maybe there is some value* in making the exercise compulsory, but I'll have to collect more data to find out.

Paired t-test: Exam Scores

In Fall 2016, 52 students took my first inference test exam in ISAT 251. The students who completed worksheets prior to the first exam scored better than the ones who did not. For the second exam, I forced *everyone* to complete the worksheets. I found that there was no difference in the scores between the two groups from the second exam. After all the scores were in, I wanted to know: **In general, did the students improve from Exam 1 to Exam 2?** I wouldn't be able to determine whether the intervention had a direct effect on the scores (for that, I would have needed to design an experiment and include a control group), but I could find out whether there was an improvement.

Before analyzing the data, I added a column to my data to reflect the difference in scores for each student. Negative values in the `exam.diff` column indicate that the students did *worse* on Exam 2, but positive values show that they improved.

```
> scores <-
read.csv("https://docs.google.com/spreadsheets/d/1lyqbeRdZayUrZrXD7X0__tx5WrXgNlbE9S10
6lBNS6o/pub?gid=0&single=true&output=csv",header=TRUE)
> head(scores)
  student     exam1 pass worksheets num.wkshts exam2 exam.diff
1       1        88    Y          Y          6    85        -3
2       2        90    Y          Y          5    90         0
3       3        57    N          N          0    91        34
4       4        70    N          N          0    77         7
5       5        72    N          N          0    82        10
6       6        87    Y          Y          3    89         2
```

First, let's gather the information that we'll need to calculate the test statistic, and check out a histogram of the differences in that last column:

```
> mean(scores$exam.diff)
[1] 6.038462
> sd(scores$exam.diff)
[1] 12.65835
> hist(scores$exam.diff, col="lightblue")
```

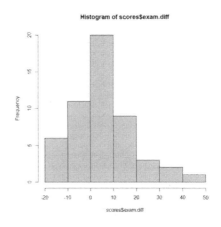

Step 0: Check Assumptions

- **Random sample** - It's not technically a random sample, because we have a score for each person in the class. But we can consider that the group of students who took this exam are a random sample of all students - in all semesters - who have, or will, take this exam. ✔
- **Observations are independent** - Does one person's exam score influence another person's exam score? Hopefully not. (That would probably be cheating.) ✔
- **Sample is small enough** - Is our sample of n=52 students less that 10% of the size of the entire population? Yes, I definitely expect that at least 520 students will be taking this exam at some time. ✔
- **Sample is large enough, or distributions are nearly normal** - The histogram for all 52 students' differences between first and second exam is approximately bell shaped. ✔

Step 1: Set Null (H₀) & Alternative (Hₐ) Hypotheses:

H₀:	$d = d_0$	d_0 is the difference you *think* exists between the first and second observation. We set $d_0 = 0$ because we just want to see if students improve *at all* -- we don't care how many points they improved. If we did, we would set d_0 equal to *that* improvement target.
Hₐ:	$d > d_0$	Then, PICK ONE version from the alternatives. From the data,
	$d < d_0$	it looks like there may have been an improvement, so let's pick
	$d \neq d_0$	the first ("greater than") option for our alternative hypothesis.

Step 2: Set α, the Level of Significance:

An **α of 0.05** means that **1 out of every 20 times** we collect data to run this test, we accept that we will *reject the null hypothesis* when that's the wrong answer. Is this OK? There are three things we have to consider: **cost** of getting new data, the **risk** of making an incorrect decision based on this test, and the **ethical considerations** associated with someone else using our results to make *their* decisions.

- First, does it cost a lot to get more data? The answer is **yes**. This test requires test scores from *two* different points in time, and a study period in between, which means that gathering new data would take lots of time and effort.
- Second, what decision will I make based on this test? If the scores show improvement, then I will have more evidence that compelling the students to do 6-8 more hours of work prior to

the exam was worth it - and I'll keep asking future students to make that investment. So the risk of making an incorrect decision is pretty significant for those future students.

- Finally, will anyone else be using my data or analysis to make *their* decisions? No. This is just for my personal use as an instructor... no one will be making policy decisions based on my test.

I might want to consider setting **α** to **0.01,** meaning that I'll make the wrong decision only **1 out of every 100 times** I potentially collect data. That seems more reasonable to me for this test. There's a lot on the line... for the workloads and stress levels of my future students.

Step 3: Calculate Test Statistic (T.S.)

This is a paired t-test, so the test statistic we want to compute is a **t.** (This also means we will use the t distribution, which is almost identical to the bell-shaped normal distribution). We know the mean difference (the mean of the `exam.diff` column), we know that d_0 is 0, we know the standard deviations of the `exam.diff` column, and we know how many items are in each group (n) so this is just a matter of plugging values in:

$$t = \frac{\bar{d} - d_0}{SE(\bar{d})} = \frac{\bar{d} - d_0}{s_d / \sqrt{n}}$$

$$t = \frac{\bar{d} - d_0}{SE(\bar{d})} = \frac{6.04}{12.66 / \sqrt{52}} = 3.45$$

Step 4: Draw a Picture

The value of t that we calculated is t=+3.45. This is far to the right of the mean in the distribution that we're using to represent our null hypothesis. By making an arrow out of the sign in our alternative hypothesis, we know to shade the area to the right of t=+3.45. The picture shows the area we will be trying to find in Step 5, which is less than 0.3% if we consider the 68-95-99.7 rule.

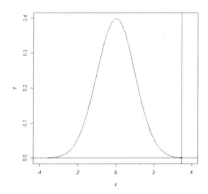

Here's the code that produced this plot (which is not shaded because the area in the tail is so tiny).

```
x <- seq(-4,4,0.1)
y <- dnorm(x)
plot(x,y,type="l")
abline(h=0)
abline(v=+3.45)
```

Step 5: Calculate P-Value

From Step 4, we estimated that the total area (our P-value) will be approximately 0%. Now let's find out exactly how large the shaded area is. Due to symmetry, the area of the tail left of t=-3.45 is the same as the area in the tail to the right of t=+3.45. We will look up the left area:

```
> pt(-3.45,df=51)
[1] 0.0005668944
```

Because our sample size is large enough, we could have used the normal distribution as an approximation to the t distribution to look up this area. There's no appreciable difference between areas that are this tiny.

```
> pnorm(-3.45)
[1] 0.0002802933
```

Step 6: Draw Conclusion

Is the P-Value < α? If so, reject the null hypothesis (H₀).

Is 0.0005 < 0.01? **Yes it is.** We **reject** the null hypothesis (H₀) that the average difference in scores is zero. **We have evidence that, on average, performance improved between Exam 1 and Exam 2.**

Let's double check in R. The syntax to run this test is **exactly the same as for the Two-Sample T-test**... the ONLY difference is that you add paired=TRUE as an argument. Also make sure that you specify your "AFTER" data first, like this:

```
> t.test(scores$exam2, scores$exam1, alternative="greater", paired=TRUE)


        Paired t-test

data:  scores$exam2 and scores$exam1
t = 3.4399, df = 51, p-value = 0.0005842
alternative hypothesis: true difference in means is greater than 0
95 percent confidence interval:
3.097671      Inf
sample estimates:
mean of the differences
            6.038462
```

Step 7: Compute Confidence Interval & Double Check in R

Always start with the general form of the confidence interval (that is, write these words):

CI: Estimate ± Margin of Error

Next, replace those words with the values you'll need to look up or calculate:

CI: (Mean of your differences) ± t$_{df}$* (Standard Error of the difference)

CI: mean(scores$diff) ± t$_{df}$* (Standard Error of the difference)

First, we compute the standard error of the difference (the denominator from when we calculated our test statistic t):

```
> 12.66/sqrt(52)
[1] 1.755626
```

And then we can multiply it by the critical t (t_{df}*) that we look up using the `qt` function, then finally use that margin of error (ME) to find the lower and upper bounds of the confidence interval:

```
> ME <- qt(0.975,df=51) * 1.76
> 6.04 + c(-ME,+ME)
[1] 2.506653 9.573347
```

We are 95% confident that the true improvement in scores between Exam 1 and Exam 2 is somewhere between 2.51 and 9.57 points. Notice how the value zero is *not* in that confidence interval? Out of all the possible improvements for scores across the population, zero is not one of the possible values. And this agrees with our hypothesis test too... we rejected the null hypothesis that there was no difference between the exam scores. Finally, check the computation of the confidence interval. Remember to **drop** `alternative="greater"` to correctly compute the confidence interval:

```
> t.test(scores$exam2, scores$exam1, paired=TRUE)


        Paired t-test

data:  scores$exam2 and scores$exam1
t = 3.4399, df = 51, p-value = 0.001168
alternative hypothesis: true difference in means is not equal to 0
95 percent confidence interval:
2.514355 9.562568
sample estimates:
mean of the differences
            6.038462
```

Paired t-test: Gas Mileage

You've discovered a fuel additive that claims to improve your gas mileage by *at least* 5 mpg. To test this claim, you measure the gas mileage for 16 cars both *before* and *after* you combine the additive with a full tank of gas. You work for a car dealership, so you were able to get a random sample of 16 of the same type of late-model cars that came through your lot last month.

```
> mpg.before <- c(25,21,18,19,29,30,16,12,15,19,18,15,25,28,21)
> mpg.after  <- c(27,22,20,19,28,27,19,15,16,19,19,16,27,27,22)
> hist(mpg.after-mpg.before,col="lightblue")
> mean(mpg.after-mpg.before)
[1] 0.8
> sd(mpg.after-mpg.before)
[1] 1.612452
```

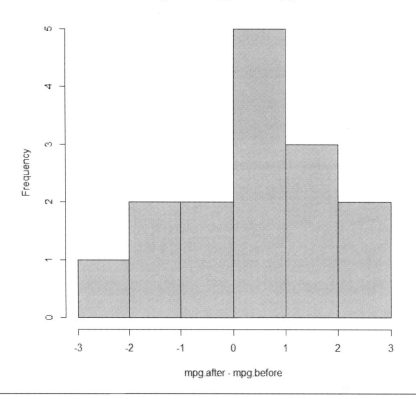

Histogram of mpg.after - mpg.before

Step 0: Check Assumptions

- **Random sample** - We are told that this is a random sample. ☑
- **Observations are independent** - The gas mileage in one car is definitely not going to influence the gas mileage from another car, so our observations are independent. (In the future, when all cars are connected, this might not be a viable assumption. But for now, it holds.) ☑
- **Sample is small enough** - Is our sample of n=15 cars less than 10% of the size of the entire population of cars that come through our lot? Yes, we have about 2500 cars pass through our lot each month. ☑
- **Sample is large enough, or distributions are nearly normal** - The histogram for all 16 cars' mileage differences between first and second assessment is approximately bell shaped. ☑

Step 1: Set Null (H_o) & Alternative (H_a) Hypotheses:

H_0: $d = d_0$ d_0 is the difference you *think* exists between the first and second observation. We set $d_0 = 0$ because we just want to see if gas mileage improves *at all* -- we don't care by how many miles per gallon. If we did, we would set $d_0 = $ *that* improvement target. We can test the claim the manufacturer makes by setting $d_0 = 5$ mpg.

H_a: $d > d_0$ Next, we PICK ONE version from the alternatives. We want to see
           $d < d_0$ if gas mileage improves, so let's pick the **first option** for our
           $d \neq d_0$ alternative hypothesis.

Step 2: Set α, the Level of Significance:

An **α of 0.05** means that **1 out of every 20 times** we collect data to run this test, we accept that we will *reject the null hypothesis* when that's the wrong answer. Is this OK? There are three things we have to consider: **cost** of getting new data, the **risk** of making an incorrect decision based on this test, and the **ethical considerations** associated with someone else using our results to make *their* decisions.

- First, does it cost a lot to get more data? The answer is **yes**. We need to drive a car through a whole tank of gas for each before and after data point.
- Second, what decision will I make based on this test? We may choose to fill the tanks of the cars we sell, and include the additive (presumably, to encourage people to continue buying it

from us). This will impact our bottom line, so we don't want to take that step if the additive is ineffective.

- Finally, will anyone else be using my data or analysis to make *their* decisions? No. This is just for our own use as a company... no one will be making policy decisions based on this test.

Another consideration is that the customers might feel as if they are receiving something special if we give them free fuel additive for their car, which wouldn't hurt (even if the additive has no demonstrable impact on the gas mileage.) As a result, although we *could* make the alpha more stringent, **let's keep it at 0.05**. If we reject the null hypothesis when we really should not have done this (that is, when the null hypothesis that there is no difference in gas mileage is actually true) our customers will still feel more special.

Step 3: Calculate Test Statistic (T.S.)

This is a paired t-test, so the test statistic we want to compute is a **t**. (This also means we will use the t distribution, which is almost identical to the bell-shaped normal distribution). We know the mean difference (0.8), we know that d_0 is 0, we know the standard deviations of differences (1.61), and we know how many items are in each group (16) so this is just a matter of plugging values in:

$$t = \frac{\bar{d} - d_0}{SE(\bar{d})} = \frac{\bar{d} - d_0}{s_d / \sqrt{n}}$$

$$t = \frac{\bar{d} - d_0}{SE(\bar{d})} = \frac{0.8}{1.61 / \sqrt{15}} = 1.92$$

Step 4: Draw a Picture

The value of t that we calculated is t=+1.92. This is to the right of the mean in the distribution that we're using to represent our null hypothesis. By making an arrow out of the sign in our alternative hypothesis, we know to shade the area to the right of t=+1.92. The picture shows the area we will be trying to find in Step 5, which is slightly larger than 2.5% if we consider the 68-95-99.7 rule.

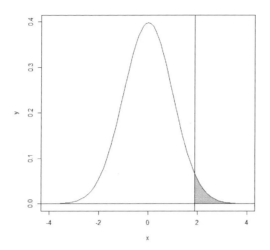

Here's the code that produced this plot:

```
> x <- seq(-4,4,0.1)
> y <- dnorm(x)
> plot(x,y,type="l")
> abline(h=0)
> abline(v=+1.9)
> which(x=="1.9")   # Approximate 1.92 with 1.9, since we plotted in tenths
[1] 60
> length(x)
[1] 81
> 81-60+1
[1] 22
> polygon(c(x[60:81],rev(x[60:81])), c(rep(0,22),rev(y[60:81])), col="lightgray")
```

Step 5: Calculate P-Value

From Step 4, we estimated that the total area (our P-value) will be approximately 2.5%. Now let's find out exactly how large the shaded area is. Due to symmetry, the area of the tail left of t=-1.99 is the same as the area in the tail to the right of t=+1.99. Degrees of freedom are calculated as (number of pairs) - 1 = 14. We will look up the left area:

```
> pt(-1.92,df=14)
[1] 0.03773397
```

Step 6: Draw Conclusion

Is the P-Value < α? If so, reject the null hypothesis (H₀).

Is 0.037 < 0.05? **Yes it is, just by a little.** We **reject** the null hypothesis (H₀) that there is no gas mileage improvement. We have evidence that, on average, gas mileage improved when the additive was added... but the evidence is not strong at all.

Let's double check in R. The syntax to run this test is **exactly the same as for the Two-Sample t-test**... the ONLY difference is that we add `paired=TRUE` as an argument. Also make sure that you specify your "AFTER" data first, like this:

```
> t.test(mpg.after,mpg.before,paired=TRUE,alternative="greater")


        Paired t-test

data:  mpg.after and mpg.before
t = 1.9215, df = 14, p-value = 0.03763
alternative hypothesis: true difference in means is greater than 0
95 percent confidence interval:
0.06670812          Inf
sample estimates:
mean of the differences
                  0.8
```

Step 7: Compute Confidence Interval & Double Check in R

Always start with the general form of the confidence interval (that is, write these words):

CI: Estimate ± Margin of Error

Next, replace those words with the values you'll need to look up or calculate:

CI: (Mean of your differences) ± t_{df}* (Standard Error of the difference)

CI: mean(mpg.after - mpg.before) ± t_{df}* (Standard Error of the difference)

First, we compute the Standard Error of the difference (the denominator from when we calculated our test statistic t):

```
> 1.61/sqrt(15)
[1] 0.4157002
```

Next, multiply it by the critical t ($t_{df}*$) that we look up using the `qt` function, then finally use that margin of error (ME) to find the lower and upper bounds of the 95% confidence interval:

```
> ME <- qt(0.975,df=14) * 0.4157
> 0.8 + c(-ME,ME)
[1] -0.09158783  1.69158783
```

We are 95% confident that the true improvement in gas mileage with the additive is somewhere between -0.09 and 1.69 miles per gallon. Notice how the value **zero** lies within that confidence interval? Out of all the possible improvements for scores across the population, zero is a distinct possibility. Remember when we rejected the null hypothesis, but only barely? This confidence interval corroborates this conclusion.

Finally, check the confidence interval. Remember to **drop** the `alternative="greater"` **part** if you want to correctly compute the confidence interval:

```
> t.test(mpg.after,mpg.before,paired=TRUE)

        Paired t-test

data:  mpg.after and mpg.before
t = 1.9215, df = 14, p-value = 0.07526
alternative hypothesis: true difference in means is not equal to 0
95 percent confidence interval:
-0.0929459  1.6929459
sample estimates:
mean of the differences
               0.8
```

Paired t-test: Shrinking People

Did you know that when you sleep, your spinal column relaxes and expands? Then, when you go about your daily business, the effect of gravity (and carrying heavy objects) can compress your spine to such an extent that you actually *lose height* from the beginning of the day to the end of the day. We measured the heights of 13 students in our class in mm upon awakening, and upon going to sleep. **Are students shorter at night?**

```
am <- c(1524,1610,1660,1828,1800,1590,1710,1750,1800,1548,1643,1669,1890)
pm <- c(1521,1610,1650,1815,1801,1580,1708,1749,1802,1540,1640,1668,1890)
```

First, let's gather the information that we'll need to calculate the test statistic, and check out a histogram of the differences in that last column:

```
> hist(am-pm,main="Histogram of Differences",col="lightblue")
```

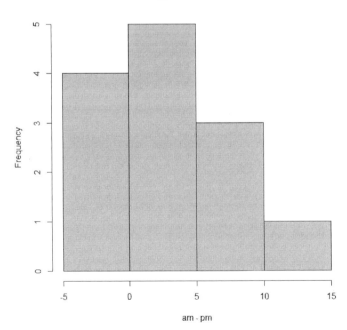

Step 0: Check Assumptions

- **Random sample** - It's not technically a random sample, it's just a convenience sample - we measured the heights of *just* the people in our class. So if we were doing this for real research purposes, we would want to make sure we devised an appropriate sampling strategy to ensure that we have a random and representative sample. For the purpose of this research question, we'll proceed even though we don't quite meet the requirement of a random sample. ☑

- **Observations are independent** - Does one person's height difference influence another's? Definitely not, so observations are clearly independent. ☑

- **Sample is small enough** - Is our sample of n=13 people less that 10% of the size of the entire population of students? Yes, I definitely expect that at least 130 students are enrolled at our school. ☑

- **Sample is large enough, or differences are nearly normal** - The histogram for all 13 peoples' height differences between AM and PM is approximately bell shaped. So even though the sample is not large enough, we pass this assumption on the basis of the distribution's shape. ☑

- **Data are paired** - I have one measurement in the AM bag and another measurement in the PM bag for each person. ☑

Step 1: Set Null (H₀) & Alternative (Hₐ) Hypotheses:

H_0:	$d = d_0$	d_0 is the difference you *think* exists between the first and second observation. We will set $d_0 = 0$ because we just want to see if there is *any* height difference at all.
H_a:	$d > d_0$	Next, we PICK ONE version from the alternatives. Since we want
	$d < d_0$	to know if AM heights are **greater**, we choose the first (greater
	$d \neq d_0$	than) option.

In research reports and on exams, you should write the null and alternative with the d_0 filled in:

H_0: $d = 0$
H_a: $d > 0$

Step 2: Set α, the Level of Significance:

An **α of 0.05** means that **1 out of every 20 times** we collect data to run this test, we accept that we will *reject the null hypothesis* when that's the wrong answer. Is this OK? There are three things we have to consider: **cost** of getting new data, the **risk** of making an incorrect decision based on this test, and the **ethical considerations** associated with someone else using our results to make *their* decisions.

- First, does it cost a lot to get more data? The answer is **sort of**. We may have to recruit participants and pay them a stipend. We have to invest a bit of time and effort to make sure we are with these people when they wake up, and when they fall asleep, so that we get good measurements.
- Second, what decision will I make based on this test? Nothing critical. I just want to satisfy my curiosity.
- Finally, will anyone else be using my data or analysis to make *their* decisions? No. This is just for my personal use... no one will be making policy decisions based on my test.

We will keep the level of significance at **0.05** since the stakes are not that high.

Step 3: Calculate Test Statistic (T.S.)

This is a paired t-test, so the test statistic we want to compute is a **t.** (This also means we will use the t distribution, which is almost identical to the bell-shaped normal distribution, but has longer tails and a peakier peak). We know the mean difference (3.69), we know that d_0 is 0, we know the standard deviation of the difference (4.87), and we know how many items are in each group (n=13) so this is just a matter of plugging values in:

$$ t = \frac{\bar{d} - d_0}{SE(\bar{d})} = \frac{\bar{d} - d_0}{s_d / \sqrt{n}} $$

$$ t = \frac{\bar{d} - d_0}{SE(\bar{d})} = \frac{3.69}{4.87 / \sqrt{13}} = 2.73 $$

Step 4: Draw a Picture

The value of t that we calculated is t=+2.73. This is far to the right of the mean in the distribution that we're using to represent our null hypothesis. By making an arrow out of the sign in our alternative hypothesis, we know to shade the area to the right of t=+2.73. The picture shows the area we will be trying to find in Step 5, which should be less than 5% if we consider the 68-95-99.7 rule.

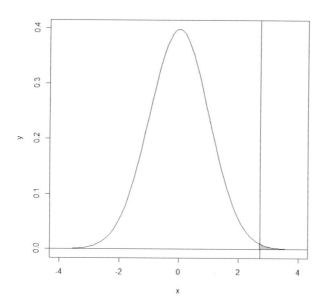

Here's the code that produced this plot:

```
> x <- seq(-4,4,0.1)
> y <- dnorm(x)
> plot(x,y,type="l")
> abline(h=0)
> abline(v=+2.73)
> which(x=="2.7")
[1] 68
> length(x)
[1] 81
> 81-68+1
[1] 14
> polygon(c(x[68:81],rev(x[68:81])), c(rep(0,14),rev(y[68:81])), col="lightgray")
```

Step 5: Calculate P-Value

From Step 4, we estimated that the total area (our P-value) will be less than 5%. Now let's find out exactly how large the shaded area is. Due to symmetry, the area of the tail left of t=-2.73 is the same as the area in the tail to the right of t=+2.73. We will look up the left area:

```
> pt(-2.73,df=12)
[1] 0.009133247
```

Step 6: Draw Conclusion

Is the P-Value < α? If so, reject the null hypothesis (H$_0$).

Is 0.009 < 0.05? **Yes it is.** We **reject** the null hypothesis (H$_0$) that there is no difference in height between morning and night. It does indeed appear that people are taller when they wake up, and shrink throughout the day. Let's double check in R. The syntax to run this test is **exactly the same as for the Two-Sample t-test**... the ONLY difference is that you add `paired=TRUE` as an argument:

```
> t.test(am,pm,paired=TRUE,alternative="greater")


        Paired t-test

data:  am and pm
t = 2.7328, df = 12, p-value = 0.009085
alternative hypothesis: true difference in means is greater than 0
95 percent confidence interval:
1.284277        Inf
sample estimates:
mean of the differences
            3.692308
```

Step 7: Calculate Confidence Interval & Double Check in R

Always start with the general form of the confidence interval (that is, write these words):

CI: Estimate ± Margin of Error

Next, replace those words with the values you'll need to look up or calculate:

CI: (Mean of the Differences) ± t$_{df}$* (Standard Error of the Differences)

CI: `mean(am-pm)` ± t$_{df}$* **(Standard Error of the Differences)**

First, we compute the Standard Error of the Differences (the denominator from when we calculated our test statistic t):

```
> 4.87/sqrt(13)
[1] 1.350695
```

Next, multiply it by the critical t (t$_{df}$*) that we look up using the `qt` function, then finally use that margin of error (ME) to find the lower and upper bounds of the confidence interval:

```
> ME <- qt(0.975,df=12) * 1.35
> 3.69 + c(-ME,+ME)
[1] 0.7486027 6.6313973
```

We are 95% confident that the true height shrinkage is somewhere between 0.75 and 6.63 mm. Notice how the value zero is *not* in that confidence interval? Out of all the possible changes in height, zero is not one of the possible values. And this agrees with our hypothesis test too… we rejected the null hypothesis that there was no difference in heights. Finally, check the computation of the confidence interval. Remember to **drop** the `alternative="greater"` to correctly compute the confidence interval:

```
> t.test(am,pm,paired=TRUE)


        Paired t-test

data:  am and pm
t = 2.7328, df = 12, p-value = 0.01817
alternative hypothesis: true difference in means is not equal to 0
95 percent confidence interval:
0.7485358 6.6360796
sample estimates:
mean of the differences
          3.692308
```

One-Way ANOVA: Jimmy's Delivery Times

Jimmy's has been getting a lot of complaints lately that some deliveries are not as "lightning fast" as customers expect. Because you are now the manager at Jimmy's, and because you know how to answer research questions using statistical inference, you've decided to answer the question: **Is one of my delivery drivers taking too much time?** The data was published to the web from Google Docs as CSV, so we can read it in directly. Next, we use the `head` command to check and make sure it arrived, and then use the `levels` command to see who all the drivers are:

```
> food <-
read.csv("https://docs.google.com/spreadsheets/d/1iWIcDWCLSHDH0F8nX8KyN2mBntjjWGvGpDPW
84rocI8/pub?gid=0&single=true&output=csv")
> head(food)
  driver deliv.time
1    Joe         10
2 Alison         11
3   Kyle         13
4  Grant         15
5   Anna         16
6    Joe          7
> levels(food$driver)
[1] "Alison" "Anna"   "Grant"  "Joe"    "Kyle"
```

For this analysis, we will have **FIVE BAGS OF DATA**: one for each driver. We are testing to see if the delivery times are different for the different drivers, and in particular, if one (or more) of the drivers are taking too long. (Even though it's recommended that you have the same number of values in each bag, ANOVA usually works even if you don't. Fortunately, we have 8 observations for each driver.)

BAG #1
contains n pieces of
quantitative data

BAG #2
contains n pieces of
(the same)
quantitative data
but from a different <u>category</u>

BAG #3
contains n pieces of
(the same)
quantitative data
but from a different <u>category</u>

First, let's gather the information that we'll need to calculate the test statistic using `aggregate`, and check out a `boxplot` of the times, groupd by driver. I removed all the warnings (there were lots):

```
> aggregate(food$deliv.time, by=list(food$driver), FUN=mean)  # Calculate the MEANS
  Group.1      x
1  Alison  9.750
2    Anna 11.125
3   Grant 13.625
4     Joe 10.125
5    Kyle 11.250
> aggregate(food$deliv.time, by=list(food$driver), FUN=sd)  # Calculate the SDs
  Group.1      x
1  Alison 1.982062
2    Anna 2.695896
3   Grant 1.922610
4     Joe 1.885092
5    Kyle 1.752549
> aggregate(food$deliv.time, by=list(food$driver), FUN=length)  # Calculate the Ns
  Group.1 x
1  Alison 8
2    Anna 8
3   Grant 8
4     Joe 8
5    Kyle 8
> boxplot(deliv.time ~ driver, data=food)
```

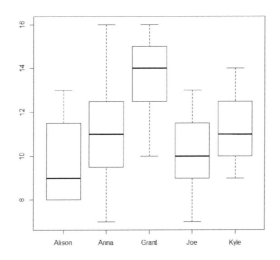

Step 0: Check Assumptions

- **Random sample** - This is a random sample of all these drivers' delivery times. We selected two times at random from the past four days of work. ✓
- **Observations are independent** - Does one driver's times affect another driver's times? I guess that's possible, but I can't think of why it might happen in this case. ✓
- **Homogeneity of variances** - Are the variances of each of the groups the same? By looking at the boxplot, we see that the variances are very similar. ✓
- **Response variable is normally distributed** - From the boxplot, we see that the distributions appear to be nearly normal: the bottom half of each box is about the same size as the top half of each box. ✓
- **Size of groups is the same** - Our groups contain 8 observations each. ✓

Step 1: Set Null (H₀) & Alternative (Hₐ) Hypotheses:

For one-way ANOVA, the null and alternative hypothesis are **always the same**... the only thing that you need to change is the number of means in your H_0 (because it needs to match the number of bags of data you have). Since we have five bags, we have five μ's... one for each driver.

H_0: $\mu_{Alison} = \mu_{Anna} = \mu_{Grant} = \mu_{Joe} = \mu_{Kyle}$

H_a: At least one of the means is different than the others.

Just from looking at our boxplot, it seems like maybe Grant is the slow one. But our statistical analysis will tell us for sure.

Step 2: Set α, the Level of Significance:

An **α of 0.05** means that **1 out of every 20 times** we collect data to run this test, we accept that we will *reject the null hypothesis* when that's the wrong answer. Is this OK? There are three things we have to consider: **cost** of getting new data, the **risk** of making an incorrect decision based on this test, and the **ethical considerations** associated with someone else using our results to make *their* decisions.

- First, does it cost a lot to get more data? The answer is **no**. I have a lot of drivers, and they make a lot of deliveries each day.

- Second, what decision will I make based on this test? None yet, but if I find that one driver is consistently slow, then I might need to provide that driver with additional training. If that doesn't work, then I might need to fire that driver. Either way, the consequences are high.
- Finally, will anyone else be using my data or analysis to make *their* decisions? No, just me.

As a result, let's make our alpha a little more stringent, and **set it to 0.01**. That means that we're willing to reject the null hypothesis -- we're willing to *call out one of our employees for unacceptable performance* even if they really are doing a good job overall -- only 1 in 100 times. (If it was you, wouldn't you want us to make our decision on this more stringent alpha?)

Step 3: Calculate Test Statistic (T.S.) in R

This is a one-way ANOVA, so the test statistic we want to compute is an **F**. (This also means we will use the F distribution, which peaks early and has a long tail to the right). We will **only** do this test in R because calculations are labor intensive. Running `aov` generates the ANOVA table for the response variable (`food$deliv.time`) split up into groups by ("~") driver (`food$driver`) :

```
> model <- aov(deliv.time ~ driver, data=food)
> summary(model)
            Df Sum Sq Mean Sq F value  Pr(>F)
driver       4  73.15  18.287   4.249 0.00659 **
Residuals   35 150.62   4.304
---
Signif. codes:  0 '***' 0.001 '**' 0.01 '*' 0.05 '.' 0.1 ' ' 1
```

Step 4: Draw a Picture

The value of t that we calculated is F=+4.249. This is far to the right on our distribution. The picture shows the area we will be trying to find in Step 5, which is really big: probably close to 100%.

Here's the code that produced the plot on the next page. We didn't even shade the area because it's so tiny.

```
x <- seq(0,3,0.01)
y <- df(x,4,36) # Numerator is 3 (groups - 1); Denominator is 27 (total obs -
groups)
plot(x,y,type="l")
abline(h=0)
abline(v=+4.249)
```

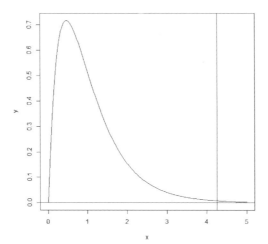

Step 5: Calculate P-Value

From Step 4, we estimated that the total area (our P-value) will be approximately 80-90%. Now let's find out exactly how large the shaded area is. R always looks up areas to the left, but we need the area to the right of the vertical line at F=0.118. To get this value, we also need to provide a "numerator degrees of freedom" (which is the **number of groups minus one**; in this case, 4-3=1) and the "denominator degrees of freedom" (which is **total number of observations minus number of groups**, or 31-4=27):

```
> 1-pf(4.249,4,36)
[1] 0.006424344
```

Step 6: Draw Conclusion

Is the P-Value < α? If so, reject the null hypothesis (H₀).

Is 0.006 < 0.01? **Yes it is!** We **reject** the null hypothesis (H₀) that the drivers have the same average delivery time. Our data suggests that at least one of the drivers' average times is different. **But who?**

Step 7: Confidence Intervals and Tukey's HSD Test

If we rejected the null hypothesis, and we knew that at least one bag of data had a different mean, how would we know **which one was higher or lower** than the others? To do this, you have to run a post hoc test like Tukey's Honestly Significant Differences (HSD). This compares the mean of every bag to the mean of every other bag, in a pairwise manner, so we end up getting confidence intervals for the difference between means in each pair of bags:

```
> TukeyHSD(model)
  Tukey multiple comparisons of means
    95% family-wise confidence level

Fit: aov(formula = deliv.time ~ driver, data = food)


$driver
               diff        lwr        upr      p adj
Anna-Alison    1.375 -1.6071637  4.3571637 0.6774553
Grant-Alison   3.875  0.8928363  6.8571637 0.0056319   <- this one is significant!
Joe-Alison     0.375 -2.6071637  3.3571637 0.9961752
Kyle-Alison    1.500 -1.4821637  4.4821637 0.6029992
Grant-Anna     2.500 -0.4821637  5.4821637 0.1364255
Joe-Anna      -1.000 -3.9821637  1.9821637 0.8692540
Kyle-Anna      0.125 -2.8571637  3.1071637 0.9999499
Joe-Grant     -3.500 -6.4821637 -0.5178363 0.0146889   <- this one is significant!
Kyle-Grant    -2.375 -5.3571637  0.6071637 0.1723577
Kyle-Joe       1.125 -1.8571637  4.1071637 0.8131646
```

This is easier to interpret when you look at all of it plotted together (next page). Notice how **all of the confidence intervals but Grant-Alison and Joe-Grant have zero in them**. That means that there is no detectable difference in any of the pairs *except these two pairs with Grant*. This means that Grant is definitely slower than Alison and Joe, but we can't be sure that he's slower than Kyle or Anna.

On the plot, there are *honestly significant differences* between any of the pairs where the confidence interval *doesn't* intersect the vertical dotted zero line. The code that produced the plot on the next page is:

```
> plot(TukeyHSD(model), cex.axis=0.6, las=2)
```

(Note: the `las=2` part makes the driver's names on the left horizontal instead of vertical, and the `cex.axis=0.6` shrinks the letters to 60% of their regular size so they aren't cut off by the left side of the plot.)

95% family-wise confidence level

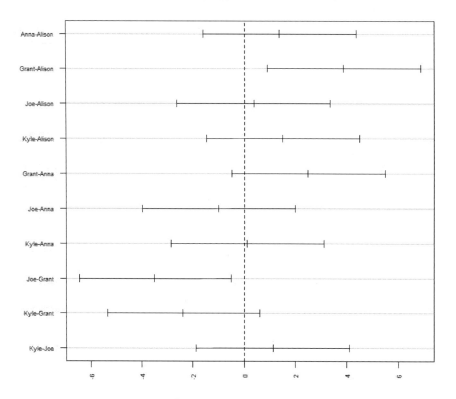

Differences in mean levels of driver

Bonus: One of the more advanced things that you do when you create ANOVA models is to check your model to make sure it's "good". For example, in the "Residuals vs Fitted" plot, you want to make sure your residuals are randomly scattered around the zero line, and that they don't show heterscedasticity (which is a megaphone-like pattern where the variation goes from small to large from left to right, or large to small from left to right). Our plots look pretty good... we have a good model.

```
> par(mfrow=c(2,2))
> plot(model)
```

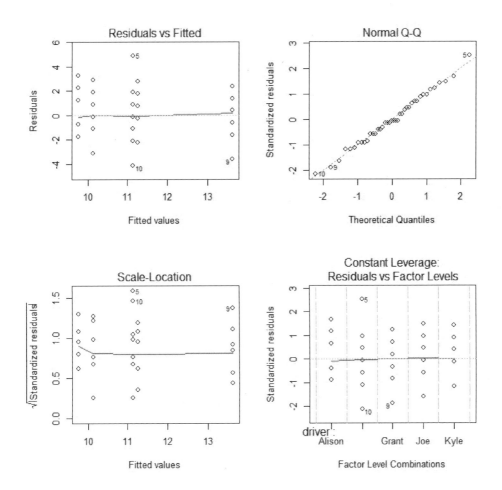

Final Note: When sample sizes are small, or assumptions don't quite all check out, consider conducting the Kruskal-Wallis test (`kruskal.test`), a nonparametric alternative to the one-way ANOVA.

One-Way ANOVA: Harrisonburg Snowfall

One of my senior capstone groups is working to improve snow forecasting for Harrisonburg. Official snow totals are recorded at the Shenandoah airport, but we've noticed that those official values don't always match up with what we observe on campus - and often, the snowfall on one side of campus is greater than the snowfall on the other side of campus. We've started collecting some data to explore the variability of snow totals. Right now, we would like to know: **Has the average daily snowfall been the same over the past 4 seasons?** There are two ways we can measure this: by looking at the actual snowfall, or by looking at the liquid equivalent (how much water there is when the snow is melted). In this example, we'll focus on the liquid equivalent.

```
> snow <-
read.csv("https://docs.google.com/spreadsheets/d/1t9z3kuKSF9t7QKRpt9me5nv7WAVcxcASTR67
DYrEf9s/pub?gid=0&single=true&output=csv")
> head(snow)
  mo da   yr season event liquid accum significant
1 Dec  8 2013      1     1   0.01  0.01           0
2 Dec 10 2013      1     2   0.23  1.40           1
3 Dec 11 2013      1     2   0.48  3.00           1
4 Dec 14 2013      1     3   0.28  0.90           0
5 Jan  3 2014      1     4   0.14  0.70           0
6 Jan 16 2014      1     5   0.08  1.20           0
```

For this analysis, we will have **FOUR BAGS OF DATA**: one for 2013, one for 2014, one for 2015, and one for 2016. We are testing to see if the liquid equivalent of the snow is the same between these four seasons, or if one of them is different. (Even though it's recommended that you have the same number of values in each bag, ANOVA usually works even if you don't.

BAG #1
contains n pieces of
quantitative data

BAG #2
contains n pieces of
(the same)
quantitative data
but from a different <u>category</u>

BAG #3
contains n pieces of
(the same)
quantitative data
but from a different <u>category</u>

First, let's gather the information that we'll need to calculate the test statistic using `aggregate`, and check out a boxplot of the liquid equivalents, grouped by year:

```
> aggregate(snow, by=list(snow$yr), FUN=mean)   # Calculate the MEANS
  Group.1 mo       da    yr season    event    liquid      accum significant
1    2013 NA 10.75000 2013 1.000000 2.000000 0.2500000 1.327500    0.5000000
2    2014 NA 15.42857 2014 1.214286 6.714286 0.4842857 3.635714    0.4285714
3    2015 NA 18.57143 2015 2.000000 5.285714 0.5042857 4.171429    0.5714286
4    2016 NA 13.16667 2016 3.000000 3.500000 0.4250000 3.435000    0.1666667
> aggregate(snow, by=list(snow$yr), FUN=sd)     # Calculate the ST DEVs
  Group.1        mo       da yr    season     event    liquid      accum significant
1    2013 0.0000000 2.500000  0 0.0000000 0.8164966 0.1930458 1.254469    0.5773503
2    2014 1.1883131 8.345559  0 0.4258153 3.6674991 0.4432869 3.895679    0.5135526
3    2015 0.7559289 9.235026  0 0.0000000 1.7994708 0.5537706 4.596634    0.5345225
4    2016 0.9831921 7.139094  0 0.0000000 1.8708287 0.7597039 6.186190    0.4082483
> aggregate(snow, by=list(snow$yr), FUN=length) # Find out how many items in each
group
  Group.1 mo da yr season event liquid accum significant
1    2013  4  4  4      4     4      4     4           4
2    2014 14 14 14     14    14     14    14          14
3    2015  7  7  7      7     7      7     7           7
4    2016  6  6  6      6     6      6     6           6
```

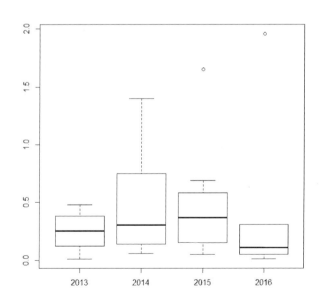

Step 0: Check Assumptions

- **Random sample** - This is not technically a random sample, because we don't have enough snow events to select a truly random sample. But for the purpose of this problem, we're going to assume that it's random enough. ✓
- **Observations are independent** - Does snowfall on one day influence the snowfall on another day? Unfortunately, yes... snow events don't care that midnight has occurred, and the total snowfall will be dependent on the physical mechanisms that caused the snowstorm. ✓
- **Homogeneity of variances** - Are the variances of each of the groups the same? By looking at the boxplot, we see that the variance in 2014 is significantly higher than the other years, and that 2015 and 2016 have some outliers. However, ANOVA is **robust** enough so that this method usually works even if the variances within the groups aren't exactly the same. ✓
- **Response variable is normally distributed** - From the boxplot, we see that the distributions appear to be nearly normal: the bottom half of each box is about the same size as the top half of each box. ✓
- **Size of groups is the same** - Our groups contain 4, 14, 7, and 6 observations, so definitely do not have the same size. However, ANOVA is also robust to violating this assumption! Doing the calculations manually is much more difficult, but R handles it well. So for the purposes of this problem, we'll move forward.

Step 1: Set Null (H₀) & Alternative (Hₐ) Hypotheses:

For one-way ANOVA, the null and alternative hypothesis are always the same... the only thing that you need to change is the number of means in your H_0 (because it needs to match the number of bags of data you have). Since we have four bags, we have four µ's... one for each season.

H_0: $\mu_{2013} = \mu_{2014} = \mu_{2015} = \mu_{2016}$
H_a: At least one of the means is different than the others.

Step 2: Set α, the Level of Significance:

An **α of 0.05** means that **1 out of every 20 times** we collect data to run this test, we accept that we will *reject the null hypothesis* when that's the wrong answer. Is this OK? There are three things we have to consider: **cost** of getting new data, the **risk** of making an incorrect decision based on this test, and the **ethical considerations** associated with someone else using our results to make *their* decisions.

- First, does it cost a lot to get more data? The answer is **yes**. We need to wait for an entire more year of snow to get a new bag of data. And some years, it doesn't snow that much... sometimes not at all!
- Second, what decision will I make based on this test? None. This test is purely to satisfy my curiosity. I just want to know if the total amount of snow is about the same from season to season.
- Finally, will anyone else be using my data or analysis to make *their* decisions? No.

As a result, let's keep our initial alpha.

Step 3: Calculate Test Statistic (T.S.) in R

This is a one-way ANOVA, so the test statistic we want to compute is an **F.** (This also means we will use the F distribution, which peaks early and has a long tail to the right). We will **only** do this test in R because the calculations are labor intensive. First, we need to make sure that R knows our year (yr) is a categorical variable (or `Factor`). Even though it looks like a number, we're using it to define the categories that are assigned to each of our bags of data.

```
> snow$yr <- as.factor(snow$yr)
```

Running the `aov` command then generates the ANOVA table. This generates an ANOVA for the response variable (`snow$liquid`) split up into groups by ("~") year (`snow$yr`) :

```
> model <- aov(snow$liquid ~ snow$yr)
> summary(model)
            Df  Sum Sq  Mean Sq  F value  Pr(>F)
snow$yr      3   0.201  0.06686   0.244   0.865
Residuals   27   7.392  0.27378
```


Step 4: Draw a Picture

The value of t that we calculated is F=+0.244. This is very close to the left side of our distribution. The picture shows the area we will be trying to find in Step 5, which will be associated with a *really big area*: definitely greater than 50%, and probably more like 80-90%.

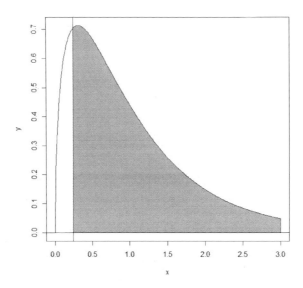

Here's the code that produced this plot, in case you want to shade an area under the F distribution.

```
x <- seq(0,3,0.01)
y <- df(x,3,27) # Numerator is 3 (groups - 1); Denominator is 27 (total obs - groups)
plot(x,y,type="l")
abline(h=0)
abline(v=+0.244)
polygon(c(x[25:301],rev(x[25:301])),c(rep(0,277),rev(y[25:301])),col="skyblue")
```

Step 5: Calculate P-Value

From Step 4, we estimated that the total area (our P-value) will be approximately 80-90%. Now let's find out exactly how large the shaded area is. R always looks up areas to the left, but we need the area to the right of the vertical line at F=0.118. To get this value, we also need to provide a "numerator degrees of freedom" (which is the number of groups minus one; in this case, 4-3=1) and the "denominator degrees of freedom" (which is total number of observations minus number of groups, or 31-4=27):

```
> 1-pf(.244,3,27)
[1] 0.8648486
```

Step 6: Draw Conclusion

Is the P-Value < α? If so, reject the null hypothesis (H₀).

Is 0.865 < 0.05? **No, it is most definitely not!** We **fail to reject** the null hypothesis (H₀) that the average liquid equivalent of snowfall is the same across the four years. We have no evidence that at least one of the years is different.

Step 7: Confidence Intervals and Tukey's HSD Test

If we rejected the null hypothesis, and we knew that at least one bag had a different mean, how would we know **which one was higher or lower** than the others? To do this, you have to run a post hoc test like Tukey's Honestly Significant Differences (HSD). This compares the mean of every bag to the mean of every other bag, in a pairwise manner, so we end up getting confidence intervals for the difference between means in each pair of bags:

```
> TukeyHSD(model)
 Tukey multiple comparisons of means
   95% family-wise confidence level

Fit: aov(formula = snow$liquid ~ snow$yr)

$`snow$yr`
                 diff        lwr        upr       p adj
2014-2013  0.23428571 -0.5775138 1.0460852 0.8584422
2015-2013  0.25428571 -0.6431924 1.1517639 0.8648788
2016-2013  0.17500000 -0.7492744 1.0992744 0.9540145
2015-2014  0.02000000 -0.6428315 0.6828315 0.9997928
2016-2014 -0.05928571 -0.7579715 0.6394001 0.9954817
2016-2015 -0.07928571 -0.8759101 0.7173386 0.9927697
```

This is easier to interpret when you look at all of it plotted together. Notice how **all of the confidence intervals have zero in them**. That means that there is no detectable difference between the liquid equivalent for the daily snowfall when any year in our sample is compared to any other year in our sample. This matches what we concluded by looking at our P-Value earlier!

```
> plot(TukeyHSD(model))
```

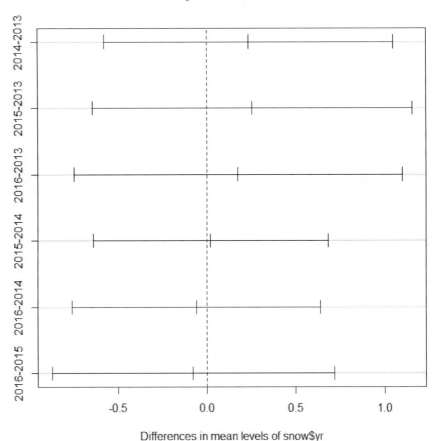

95% family-wise confidence level

Differences in mean levels of snow$yr

Bonus: One of the more advanced things that you do when you create ANOVA models is to check your model to make sure it's "good". For example, in the "Residuals vs Fitted" plot, you want to make sure your residuals are randomly scattered around the zero line, and that they don't show heterscedasticity (which is a megaphone-like pattern where the variation goes from small to large from left to right, or large to small from left to right). Unfortunately, our plot does show heteroscedasticity: the variance is small around x=0.40, and really large around x=0.50. So our model is not that great, and the P-Value is really large… affirming that there's not much interesting stuff going on with this dataset. All the snowfall totals are approximately the same, on average.

```
> par(mfrow=c(2,2))
> plot(model)
```

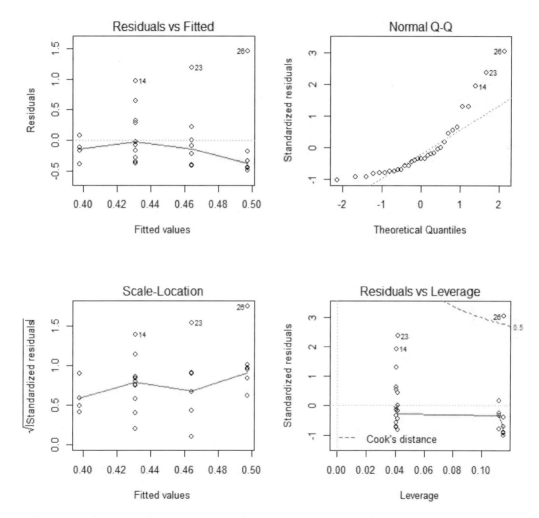

Final Note: When sample sizes are small, or assumptions don't quite all check out, consider conducting the Kruskal-Wallis test (`kruskal.test`), a nonparametric alternative to the one-way ANOVA.

One-Way ANOVA: Petal Width

R contains some "canned" datasets in the base package, in addition, many packages you install from CRAN contain data as well. This example uses the `iris` data that's already a part of the base R installation. This contains measurements made on three species of flower: `setosa`, `versicolor`, and `virginica`. Do the petal widths differ across the species? (Note: Once we complete this example, it should be easy for you to answer the exact same research question with *any* of the other three quantitative variables - sepal length, sepal width, or petal length - in place of petal width.) First let's load and look at our data, which is in a convenient data frame format.

```
> data(iris)
> head(iris)
  Sepal.Length Sepal.Width Petal.Length Petal.Width Species
1          5.1         3.5          1.4         0.2  setosa
2          4.9         3.0          1.4         0.2  setosa
3          4.7         3.2          1.3         0.2  setosa
4          4.6         3.1          1.5         0.2  setosa
5          5.0         3.6          1.4         0.2  setosa
6          5.4         3.9          1.7         0.4  setosa

> boxplot(iris$Petal.Width ~ iris$Species)
```

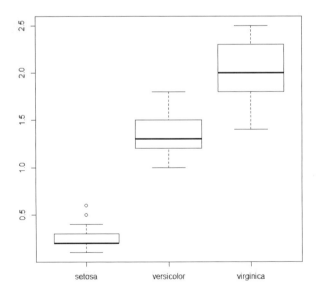

For this analysis, we will have **THREE BAGS OF DATA**: one for each species. We are testing to see if the petal widths are different for the different species, and in particular, if one (or more) of the species stand out. (Even though it's recommended that you have the same number of values in each bag, ANOVA usually works even if you don't. Fortunately, we have 50 observations for each species.)

BAG #1
contains n pieces of
quantitative data

BAG #2
contains n pieces of
(the same)
quantitative data
but from a different <u>category</u>

BAG #3
contains n pieces of
(the same)
quantitative data
but from a different <u>category</u>

Step 0: Check Assumptions

- **Random sample** - This data was gathered by a scientist who is very concerned about proper method. We can assume that the sample is random. ✔
- **Observations are independent** - Does one petal's width influence another's? Definitely not. Our observations are independent. ✔
- **Homogeneity of variances** - Are the variances of each of the groups the same? By looking at the boxplot, we see that the variance of setosa appears to be smaller. To figure out if there *really is* a difference, we have to do a test of equality of variances that works for at least three groups. Our answer is Levene's test, which can be run using leveneTest in the car package (see below). The p-value is tiny, meaning that at least one of our variances is not the same as the others. **X** However, ANOVA is fairly "robust" to violating this assumption, so we'll go ahead and proceed with the test.
- **Response variable is normally distributed** - From the boxplot, we see that the distributions appear to be nearly normal: the bottom half of each box is about the same size as the top half of each box. ✔
- **Size of groups is the same** - Our groups contain 50 observations each. ✔

```
> library(car)
> leveneTest(Petal.Width ~ Species, data=iris)
Levene's Test for Homogeneity of Variance (center = median)
      Df F value    Pr(>F)
group  2  19.892 2.261e-08 ***
      147
---
Signif. codes:  0 '***' 0.001 '**' 0.01 '*' 0.05 '.' 0.1 ' ' 1
```

Step 1: Set Null (H₀) & Alternative (Hₐ) Hypotheses:

For one-way ANOVA, the null and alternative hypothesis are **always the same**... the only thing that you need to change is the number of means in your H₀ (because it needs to match the number of bags of data you have). Since we have three bags, we have three μ's... one for each species.

H₀: $\mu_{Setosa} = \mu_{Versicolor} = \mu_{Virginica}$

Hₐ: At least one of the means is different than the others.

Just from looking at our boxplot, it seems like maybe setosa widths are smaller. But our statistical analysis will tell us for sure.

Step 2: Set α, the Level of Significance:

An **α of 0.05** means that **1 out of every 20 times** we collect data to run this test, we accept that we will *reject the null hypothesis* when that's the wrong answer. Is this OK? There are three things we have to consider: **cost** of getting new data, the **risk** of making an incorrect decision based on this test, and the **ethical considerations** associated with someone else using our results to make *their* decisions.

- First, does it cost a lot to get more data? The answer is **sort of**. We'd have to ask the researcher who collected the data, and he or she might not have any more.
- Second, what decision will I make based on this test? We're just interested in doing this test to satisfy our curiosity. There's not much riding on the outcome.
- Finally, will anyone else be using my data or analysis to make *their* decisions? No, just me.

As a result, let's go ahead and keep our alpha at **0.05**.

Step 3: Calculate Test Statistic (T.S.) in R

This is a one-way ANOVA, so the test statistic we want to compute is an **F.** (This also means we will use the F distribution, which peaks early and has a long tail to the right). We will **only** do this test in R because the calculations are labor intensive.

Running the `aov` command then generates the ANOVA table. This generates an ANOVA for the response variable (`Petal.Width`) split up into groups by ("~") species (`Species`):

```
> model <- aov(Petal.Width ~ Species, data=iris)
> summary(model)
             Df Sum Sq Mean Sq F value Pr(>F)
Species       2  80.41   40.21     960 <2e-16 ***
Residuals   147   6.16    0.04
---
Signif. codes:  0 `***' 0.001 `**' 0.01 `*' 0.05 `.' 0.1 ` ' 1
```

Step 4: Draw a Picture

The value of F that we found is F=+960. This is *so far out on the right tail* of the F distribution, we won't be able to *see* a shaded area - it will be super tiny. There is no need to even try plotting it. The area in that tail will be nearly zero.

Step 5: Calculate P-Value

From Step 4, we estimated that the total area (our P-value) will be approximately 0%. Now let's find out exactly how large the shaded area is. R always looks up areas to the left, but we need the area to the right of the vertical line at F=960. To get this value, we also need to provide a numerator degrees of freedom (which is the **number of groups minus one**; in this case, 3-1=2) and the denominator groups of freedom (which is **total number of observations minus number of groups**, or 150-3=147):

```
> 1-pf(960,2,147)
[1] 0
```

Step 6: Draw Conclusion

Is the P-Value < α? If so, reject the null hypothesis (H₀).

Is 0 < 0.05? **Yes it is!** We **reject** the null hypothesis (H₀) that the species have the same petal width. Our data suggests that at least one of the species has different dimensions. **But which one?**

If we rejected the null hypothesis, and we knew that at least one bag of data had a different mean, how would we know **which one was higher or lower** than the others? To do this, you have to run a post hoc test like Tukey's Honestly Significant Differences (HSD) test. This compares the mean of every bag to the mean of every other bag, in a pairwise manner, so we end up getting confidence intervals for the difference between means in each pair of bags:

```
> TukeyHSD(model)
  Tukey multiple comparisons of means
    95% family-wise confidence level

Fit: aov(formula = Petal.Width ~ Species, data = iris)

$Species
                      diff      lwr       upr p adj
versicolor-setosa     1.08 0.9830903 1.1769097     0
virginica-setosa      1.78 1.6830903 1.8769097     0
virginica-versicolor  0.70 0.6030903 0.7969097     0
```

The p-values above, and the plot below, show that there are significant differences in petal length between all the groups. We can't tell this *just* by rejecting our null hypothesis, but we can definitely draw this conclusion by plotting the results from the Tukey test (next page). Imagine a vertical line representing zero difference between the widths in the two groups. That vertical line is <u>far off the left of our plot</u>! A zero difference is not a possibility in any of our confidence intervals.

```
> plot(TukeyHSD(model))
```

There are significant differences between *all* our groups, which corroborates the result we got from our inference test earlier.

Bonus: One of the more advanced things that you do when you create ANOVA models is to check your model to make sure it's "good". For example, in the "Residuals vs Fitted" plot on p. 107, you want to make sure your residuals are randomly scattered around the zero line, and that they don't show heterscedasticity (which is a megaphone-like pattern where the variation goes from small to large from left to right, or large to small from left to right). Our plots look like there may be a little bit of heteroscedasticity, but our Q-Q plot looks fantastic.

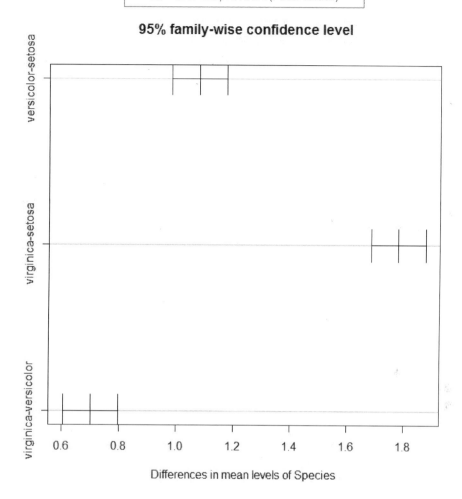

Final Note: When sample sizes are small, or assumptions don't quite all check out, consider conducting the Kruskal-Wallis test (`kruskal.test`), a nonparametric alternative to the one-way ANOVA.

```
> par(mfrow=c(2,2))
> plot(model)
```

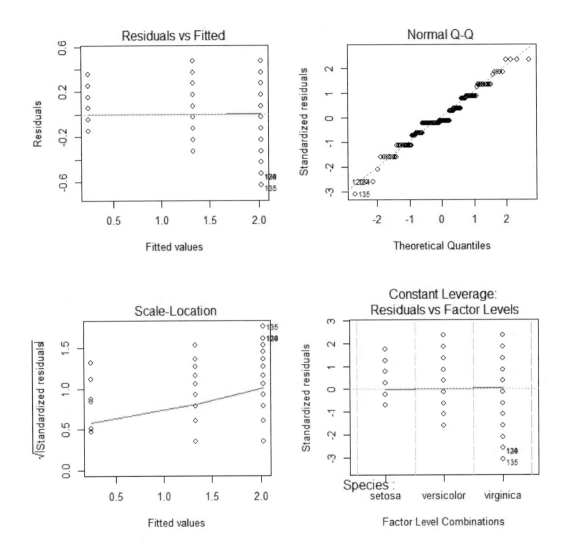

One proportion z-test: Parking

We're pretty convinced that a majority of juniors and seniors at our university are dissatisfied with the parking situation: even though everyone has to purchase a parking pass, the university tends to oversell passes, and even if you get to school on time - there's still a good chance you won't make it to class in time because you'll be circling the parking lot looking for a spot.

An enterprising group of statistics students asked 89 of their fellow students whether they were satisfied with parking. A total of 23 students were satisfied, and 66 students were dissatisfied. **Are a majority of students dissatisfied with parking?** ("Success" = "satisfied with parking")
dissatisfied

Parking Satisfaction
n = 89
x = 66
p-hat = x/n = 66/89 = 0.741
q-hat = 1 - 0.741 = 0.259

Step 0: Check Assumptions

- **Random sample** - The students used a systematic sampling strategy. We know that this is a random sample. ✔
- **Observations are independent** - Although there may be a chance that one person's satisfaction may be influenced by another's, this is unlikely. The observations appear independent. ✔
- **Sample is small enough** - Is our samples of 89 students less than 10% of the size of the entire population of university students? Yes. ✔
- **Sample is large enough** - The calculations below show that all values are greater than 10, so our sample is indeed large enough. ✔

Parking Satisfaction
n*p-hat = 89 * 0.741 = 65.95
n*q-hat = 89 * 0.259 = 22.16

Step 1: Set Null (H₀) & Alternative (Hₐ) Hypotheses:

H₀:	**p = p₀**	μ_0 is the standard, target, or recommended value. Set $p_0 = 0.50$ because if the real population proportion is above 50%, we have a majority.
Hₐ:	**p > p₀** p < p₀ p ≠ p₀	Then, we PICK ONE version from the alternatives. We want to know if *the majority* of students are dissatisfied, so pick the first ("greater than") option.

Step 2: Set α, the Level of Significance:

An **α of 0.05** means that **1 out of every 20 times** we collect data to run this test, we accept that we will *reject the null hypothesis* when that's the wrong thing to do. Is this level of significance OK? There are three things we have to consider: **cost** of getting new data, the **risk** of making an incorrect decision based on this test, and the **ethical considerations** associated with someone else using our results to make *their* decisions.

- First, does it cost a lot to get more data? No.
- Second, what decision will I make based on this test? I might decide to approach parking services and let them know they have a problem... but not this time. We only asked 89 students, so I'm considering this a pilot study.
- Finally, will anyone else be using my data or analysis to make *their* decisions? No.

As a result, let's go with an **α of 0.05.** There's not much on the line, and if we pretty much know a majority of students are dissatisfied. We will not be surprised if we reject the null hypothesis.

Step 3: Calculate Test Statistic (T.S.)

This is a one proportion z-test, so the test statistic we want to compute is a **z.** (This also means we will use the normal distribution). For the standard error, we use the p and q on the right-hand sides of our null and alternative hypotheses:

$$z = \frac{\hat{p} - p_0}{SE(\hat{p})} = \frac{\hat{p}}{\sqrt{\frac{pq}{n}}}$$

$$z = \frac{\hat{p} - p_0}{\sqrt{\frac{p_0 q_0}{n}}} = \frac{0.741 - 0.5}{\sqrt{\frac{0.5 \times 0.5}{89}}} = 4.55$$

Step 4: Draw a Picture

The value of z that we calculated is approximately z=+4.55. This is extremely far to the right of the mean in the distribution that we're using to represent our null hypothesis. By making an arrow out of the sign in our alternative hypothesis, we know to shade the area to the right of z=+4.55. We don't even need to draw the picture because the area in the tail will be so tiny... it's about zero.

Step 5: Calculate P-Value

From Step 4, we estimated that the total area (our P-value) will be 0%. Now let's find out exactly how large the shaded area is. Since R looks up the area of the left tail, we have to subtract the left tail area from 1:

```
> 1-pnorm(4.55)
[1] 2.682296e-06
```

Indeed, our p-value is 0.

Step 6: Draw Conclusion

Is the P-Value < α? If so, reject the null hypothesis (H₀).

Is 0 < 0.05? **Absolutely.** We **reject** the null hypothesis (H₀) that the proportion of dissatisfied parkers is 50%, in favor of the alternative hypothesis that the true proportion is *higher than 50%*.

Step 7: Compute Confidence Interval & Double Check in R

Always start with the general form of the confidence interval (that is, *write these words*):

CI: Estimate ± Margin of Error

Next, replace those words with the values you'll need to look up or calculate:

CI: (Sample Proportion) ± z* (Standard Error of the Proportion)

First we recall the Standard Error of the proportion (the denominator from when we calculated our test statistic z), which is 0.053. Combining this with our sample proportion (or p-hat) of 0.741, and z* = 1.96 (which hopefully you've memorized as one of the three most commonly used critical z's for confidence intervals), we get:

CI: 0.741 ± (1.96 x 0.053)

After computing the lower and upper bounds, we can say **we are 95% confident that the true proportion of students dissatisfied with parking is between 63.7% and 84.5%.** Notice how the value 50% is nowhere near this confidence interval? That tells us that 50% is *not* a possible value for the true proportion of dissatisfied parkers in the population of students.

Check Results in R

We can run this test in R to check our work. However, `prop.test` doesn't use the same equations we used to calculate our test statistic z. Instead, `prop.test` computes a *chi-square* test statistic with the Yates continuity correction, which should be a little more exact. Find out more at https://en.wikipedia.org/wiki/Yates%27s_correction_for_continuity.

We'll double check in two ways: using `z.test` (a function you can source from GitHub, that performs the same calculations that you did analytically) and also using `prop.test`. First, obtain the code for the `z.test` function:

```
source("https://raw.githubusercontent.com/NicoleRadziwill/R-
Functions/master/ztest.R")
```

Now provide your data to `z.test`. The first two numbers to provide are `x` (total number of successes) and `n` (total number of opportunities), then follow that with the proportion you are comparing your data to (p = the p_0 from your null hypothesis), and specify the alternative hypothesis (and optionally, a confidence level):

```
> z.test(66,89,p=0.50,alternative="greater")
$estimate
[1] 0.741573
```

```
$ts.z
[1] 4.557991

$p.val
[1] 2.582264e-06

$cint
[1] 0.6376952 0.8454509
```

Notice that the test statistic, P-Value, and confidence interval bounds are precisely what we found earlier when we solved analytically. Now, let's try `prop.test`:

```
> prop.test(66,89,alternative="greater",p=0.50)


        1-sample proportions test with continuity correction


data:  66 out of 89, null probability 0.5
X-squared = 19.82, df = 1, p-value = 4.254e-06
alternative hypothesis: true p is greater than 0.5
95 percent confidence interval:
0.6529574 1.0000000
sample estimates:
       p
0.741573
```

The p-value is similar to the one we got when we computed our test statistic z, and the conclusion (that we should reject the null hypothesis) remains the same. To compute the correct confidence interval, we have to drop the specification of the alternative hypothesis:

```
> prop.test(66,89,p=0.50)


        1-sample proportions test with continuity correction


data:  66 out of 89, null probability 0.5
X-squared = 19.82, df = 1, p-value = 8.508e-06
alternative hypothesis: true p is not equal to 0.5
95 percent confidence interval:
0.6359933 0.8259603
sample estimates:
       p
0.741573
```

This runs a two-tailed test - for which the null hypothesis is also rejected. *The true proportion is not 50%.* You can see in this case that the two-tailed test isn't really physically meaningful if we were trying to figure out whether a majority of students are dissatisfied. But we can read from this output that we are 95% confident that the true proportion of students who are dissatisfied with parking is between 63.6% and 82.6%. This is very close to what we found analytically earlier.

One proportion z-test: Ice Cream Sandwiches

Although you've had entrepreneurial interests for a while, you've just launched your dream company as a manufacturer of ice cream sandwiches. You bought and installed a machine that assembles the sandwiches: https://www.youtube.com/watch?v=Vlb4mfQv6-s You're not yet an expert on using the machine, and not all of the sandwiches are meeting your quality standards. Sometimes the chocolate exterior is chipped or broken, sometimes the pieces aren't exactly aligned, and sometimes (although more rarely), there's an issue with cutting or inserting the ice cream and you end up with an ice cream sandwich that just looks bad. Right now, you are aiming to have no more than 10% defective product. You systematically sampled one out of every twenty ice cream sandwiches that came off the production line today for a total of 150, and found that only 13 of them were unacceptable to offer to customers. **Are you meeting your target of having no more than 10% defective?**

Ice Cream Sandwiches
n = 150
x = 13
p-hat = x/n = 13/150 = 0.087
q-hat = 1 - 0.087 = 0.913

Step 0: Check Assumptions

- **Random sample** - We used systematic sampling to ensure that this is a random sample. ✔
- **Observations are independent** - We haven't noticed a pattern in whether a defective sandwich is more likely if it's preceded by another defective. The observations appear independent. ✔
- **Sample is small enough** - Is our sample of 150 students less than 10% of the population of ice cream sandwiches we will produce this week? Yes. ✔
- **Sample is large enough** - The calculations below show that all values are greater than 10 (even so slightly), so our sample is indeed large enough. ✔

Ice Cream Defectives
n*p-hat = 150 * 0.087 = 13.05
n*q-hat = 150 * 0.913 = 136.95

Step 1: Set Null (H₀) & Alternative (Hₐ) Hypotheses:

H₀:	**p = p₀**	p₀ is the standard, target, or recommended value. Set p₀ = 0.10
Hₐ:	**p > p₀**	Then, we PICK ONE version from the alternatives. Having fewer
	p < p₀	than 10% defective is OK… it's only a problem when *more than*
	p ≠ p₀	*that* are defective. We pick option 1.

Step 2: Set α, the Level of Significance:

An **α of 0.05** means that **1 out of every 20 times** we collect data to run this test, we accept that we will *reject the null hypothesis* when that's the wrong thing to do. Is this level of significance OK? There are three things we have to consider: **cost** of getting new data, the **risk** of making an incorrect decision based on this test, and the **ethical considerations** associated with someone else using our results to make *their* decisions.

- First, does it cost a lot to get more data? No. And we don't have to destroy or eat the ice cream sandwiches to inspect them for saleability.
- Second, what decision will I make based on this test? I might shut down my production line, even temporarily, if too many of my ice cream sandwiches can't be sold. But before I did, I would run this test again, and maybe include additional tests. I don't want to tamper with my machine unless I am absolutely sure there is special cause variation (that is, variation due to something other than random fluctuations in my production).
- Finally, will anyone else be using my data or analysis to make *their* decisions? No.

As a result, even though this is a tough decision, let's go with an **α of 0.05.** If we do reject the null hypothesis in favor of the alternative that there are more than 10% defective, our most likely plan of action will be to run the test again with a bigger sample.

Step 3: Calculate Test Statistic (T.S.)

This is a one proportion z-test, so the test statistic we want to compute is a **z.** (This also means we will use the normal distribution). For the standard error, we use the p and q on the right-hand sides of our null and alternative hypotheses:

$$z = \frac{\hat{p} - p_0}{SE(\hat{p})} = \frac{0.087 - 0.10}{\sqrt{\frac{(0.1 \times 0.9)}{150}}} = \frac{-0.013}{0.024} = -0.542$$

Step 4: Draw a Picture

The value of z that we calculated is approximately z=-0.542. This is quite a bit to the right of the mean in the distribution that we're using to represent our null hypothesis. By making an arrow out of the sign in our alternative hypothesis, we know to shade the area to the right of z=-0.542. The area will be pretty big... at least 50%, and probably between 60-70%.

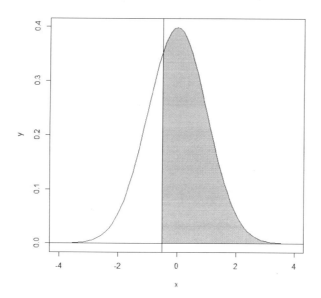

Here is the code that was used to prepare that plot:

```
> x <- seq(-4,4,0.1)
> y <- dnorm(x)
> plot(x,y,type="l")
> abline(h=0)
> abline(v=-0.5)
> which(x=="-0.5")
[1] 36
> polygon(c(x[36:81],rev(x[36:81])), c(rep(0,46),rev(y[36:81])), col="lightgray")
```

Step 5: Calculate P-Value

From Step 4, we estimated that the total area (our P-value) will be 60-70%. Now let's find out exactly how large the shaded area is. Since R looks up the area of the left tail, we have to subtract the left tail area from 1:

```
> 1-pnorm(-0.542)
[1] 0.7060907
```

Indeed, our p-value matches our estimate.

Step 6: Draw Conclusion

Is the P-Value < α? If so, reject the null hypothesis (H$_0$).

Is 0.706 < 0.05? **No way.** We **fail to reject** the null hypothesis (H$_0$) that the proportion of defective product is greater than 10%. This is good news for our fledgling ice cream sandwich factory.

Step 7: Compute Confidence Interval & Double Check in R

Always start with the general form of the confidence interval (that is, *write these words*):

CI: Estimate ± Margin of Error

Next, replace those words with the values you'll need to look up or calculate:

CI: (Sample Proportion) ± z* (Standard Error of the Proportion)

First, we recall the Standard Error of the proportion (the denominator from when we calculated our test statistic z), which is 0.024. Combining this with our sample proportion (or p-hat) of 0.087, and z* = 1.96 (which hopefully you've memorized as one of the three most commonly used critical z's for confidence intervals), we get:

CI: 0.087 ± (1.96 x 0.024)

After computing the lower and upper bounds, we can say **we are 95% confident that the true proportion of defective ice cream sandwiches is between 3.9% and 13.4%.** Notice how our target value of 10% is right in the middle of this confidence interval? That tells us that 10% is *certainly* a possible value for the true proportion of defectives in the population of all ice cream sandwiches we're making. That's why we don't reject the null hypothesis.

We can run this test in R to check our work. However, `prop.test` doesn't use the same equations we used to calculate our test statistic z. Instead, `prop.test` computes a *chi-square* test statistic with the Yates continuity correction, which should be a little more exact. Find out more at https://en.wikipedia.org/wiki/Yates%27s_correction_for_continuity.

We'll double check in two ways: using `z.test` (a function you can source from GitHub, that performs the same calculations that you did analytically) and also using `prop.test`. First, obtain the code for the `z.test` function:

```
source("https://raw.githubusercontent.com/NicoleRadziwill/R-
Functions/master/ztest.R")
```

Checking with `z.test` shows that the test statistic and confidence interval bounds are exactly what we determined analytically:

```
> z.test(13,150,p=0.10,alternative="greater")
$estimate
[1] 0.08666667

$ts.z
[1] -0.5443311

$p.val
[1] 0.7068932

$cint
[1] 0.03865755 0.13467578
```

Finally, we check with `prop.test`:

```
> prop.test(13,150,p=0.10,alternative="greater")

        1-sample proportions test with continuity correction

data:  13 out of 150, null probability 0.1
X-squared = 0.16667, df = 1, p-value = 0.6585
alternative hypothesis: true p is greater than 0.1
```

```
95 percent confidence interval:
 0.05319346 1.00000000
sample estimates:
        p
0.08666667
```

The p-value is similar to the one we got when we computed our test statistic z, and the conclusion (that we should reject the null hypothesis) remains the same. To compute the correct confidence interval, we have to drop the specification of the alternative hypothesis:

```
> prop.test(13,150,p=0.10)

        1-sample proportions test with continuity correction

data:  13 out of 150, null probability 0.1
X-squared = 0.16667, df = 1, p-value = 0.6831
alternative hypothesis: true p is not equal to 0.1
95 percent confidence interval:
 0.04884108 0.14660455
sample estimates:
        p
0.08666667
```

This runs a two-tailed test - for which the null hypothesis is also not rejected. *The true proportion could certainly be 10%.* You can see in this case that the two-tailed test isn't really physically meaningful for our manufacturing environment... there's nothing special about getting *exactly* 10% defectives in this production context. But we can say that we are 95% confident that we generate between 4.9% and 14.7% defectives. If we want to be a little more certain, run a 99% CI:

```
> prop.test(13,150,p=0.10,conf.level=0.99)

        1-sample proportions test with continuity correction

data:  13 out of 150, null probability 0.1
X-squared = 0.16667, df = 1, p-value = 0.6831
alternative hypothesis: true p is not equal to 0.1
99 percent confidence interval:
 0.0414240 0.1687742
sample estimates:
        p
0.08666667
```

Here, the confidence interval widens a bit, as we expected: we are 99% certain that the true proportion of defectives is between 4.1% and 16.9%.

One proportion z-test: the SNAP_R Phishing Utility

[Find out more about SNAP_R at https://www.blackhat.com/docs/us-16/materials/us-16-Seymour-Tully-Weaponizing-Data-Science-For-Social-Engineering-Automated-E2E-Spear-Phishing-On-Twitter.pdf]

SNAP_R is a program written to automate "spear phishing" - that is, contacting an individual online while masquerading as a "trusted source" and convincing him or her to divulge sensitive personal (or business) information. I found out about this tool watching a video from DEFCON 24, an annual hacker's conference held in Las Vegas. They provided some observations about how many times their victims clicked malicious links based on whether humans or SNAP_R were doing the phishing. The best spear phishing initiatives, they said, get a 45% click through.

We are told that **the hackers running this test convinced 275 people out of 819 to click through**, compared to 49 out of 129 when a human was doing the phishing. With this data, we can answer three research questions:

1. **Do humans get greater than 45% click-through?**
2. **Does SNAP_R get greater than 45% click-through?** (That is, does this new software effectively steal victims' personal information?)
3. **Does SNAP_R snag a greater percentage of victims than human phishers?**

We will answer the first two of these questions using the one proportion z-test. We will do #1 analytically and in R, and #2 in R only.

Human Phisher	SNAP_R Phisher
n = 129 x = 49 p-hat = x/n = 49/129 = 0.380 q-hat = 1 - 0.380 = 0.62	n = 819 x = 275 p-hat = x/n = 275/819 = 0.336 q-hat = 1 - 0.336 = 0.664

Step 0: Check Assumptions

- **Random sample** - We are told that this is a random sample. ✔
- **Observations are independent** - Although there may be a chance that one victim encouraged a friend to *also click on the phishing link*, this is unlikely. The observations appear independent. ✔

- **Sample is small enough** - Are our samples of 129 and 819 people less than 10% of the size of the entire population of phishing victims? Unfortunately, yes. ✔
- **Sample is large enough** - The probability of "success" is the probability of getting hacked, so the calculations below affirm that we have a large enough sample... all values are greater than 10. ✔

Human Phisher	SNAP_R Phisher
n*p-hat = 129 * 0.38 = 49	n*p-hat = 819 * 0.336 = 275.2
n*q-hat = 129 * 0.62 = 80	n*q-hat = 819 * 0.664 = 543.8

Step 1: Set Null (H₀) & Alternative (Hₐ) Hypotheses:

H_0: $p = p_0$ μ_0 is the standard, target, or recommended value. Set $p_0 = 0.45$

H_a: $p > p_0$ Then, PICK ONE version from the alternatives. We want to
       $p < p_0$ know if phishing is *more* effective than usual, so we choose the
       $p \neq p_0$ first ("greater than") options.

Step 2: Set α, the Level of Significance:

An **α of 0.05** means that **1 out of every 20 times** we collect data to run this test, we accept that we will *reject the null hypothesis* when that's the wrong thing to do. Is this level of significance OK? There are three things we have to consider: **cost** of getting new data, the **risk** of making an incorrect decision based on this test, and the **ethical considerations** associated with someone else using our results to make *their* decisions.

- First, does it cost a lot to get more data? Sort of. Phishing is labor intensive.
- Second, what decision will I make based on this test? I could be deciding whether to use SNAP_R for my nefarious purposes, or maybe I'm trying to decide whether to commit new resources (time, money, and labor) to the development project. Both decisions are substantial.
- Finally, will anyone else be using my data or analysis to make *their* decisions? That's definitely a possibility.

As a result, let's go with an **α of 0.01.** I'd rather only be wrong 1 out of every 100 samples I collect. Those stakes are somewhat high.

Step 3: Calculate Test Statistic (T.S.)

This is a one proportion z-test, so the test statistic we want to compute is a **z.** (This also means we will use the normal distribution). For the standard error, we use the p and q on the right-hand sides of our null and alternative hypotheses:

$$z = \frac{\hat{p} - p_0}{SE(\hat{p})} = \frac{\hat{p} - p_0}{\sqrt{\frac{pq}{n}}}$$

$$z = \frac{\hat{p} - p_0}{\sqrt{\frac{pq}{n}}} = \frac{0.38 - 0.45}{\sqrt{\frac{0.45 \times 0.55}{129}}} = -1.60$$

Step 4: Draw a Picture

The value of z that we calculated is approximately z=-1.60. This is quite a bit to the left of the mean in the distribution that we're using to represent our null hypothesis. By making an arrow out of the sign in our alternative hypothesis, we know to shade the area to the right of z=-1.60. The picture shows the area we will be trying to find in Step 5, which is definitely more than 50%.

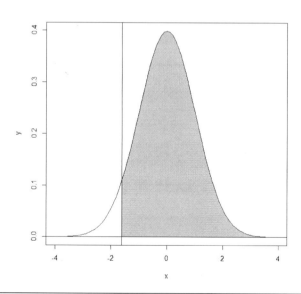

Here's the code that produced this plot:

```
x <- seq(-4,4,0.1)
y <- dnorm(x)
plot(x,y,type="l")
abline(h=0)
abline(v=-1.6)


> which(x=="-1.6")
[1] 25


polygon(c(x[25:81],rev(x[25:81])), c(rep(0,57),rev(y[25:81])), col="lightgray")
```

Step 5: Calculate P-Value

From Step 4, we estimated that the total area (our P-value) will be greater than 50%. Now let's find out exactly how large the shaded area is. Since R looks up the area of the left tail, we have to subtract the left tail area from 1:

```
> 1-pnorm(-1.6)
[1] 0.9452007
```

Not only is the area greater than 50%, it's nearly the full area under the curve.

Step 6: Draw Conclusion

Is the P-Value < α? If so, reject the null hypothesis (H₀).

Is 0.945 < 0.01? **No, it is not.** We **fail to reject** the null hypothesis (H₀) that the proportion of successfully phished accounts is 45%.

Step 7: Compute Confidence Interval & Double Check in R

Always start with the general form of the confidence interval (that is, *write these words*):

CI: Estimate ± Margin of Error

Next, replace those words with the values you'll need to look up or calculate:

CI: (Sample Proportion) ± z* (Standard Error of the Proportion)

First, we compute the Standard Error of the proportion (the denominator from when we calculated our test statistic t):

```
> sqrt((0.45*0.55)/129)
[1] 0.04380188
```

Finally, we plug in the values from our sample data, using z* = 1.96 (which hopefully you've memorized as one of the three most commonly used critical z's for confidence intervals):

CI: 0.38 ± (1.96 x 0.0438)

After computing the lower and upper bounds, we can say **we are 95% confident that the true proportion of victims who have succumbed to phishing attempts by humans is between 29.4% and 46.5%.** So there's a tiny chance that the true proportion of successes is greater than the magic level of 45%, but (unfortunately) for proportions this particular equation for the confidence interval is the least reliable. Let's use the PropCIs package to calculate more accurate CIs using the "Add 4" method and the Wilson Score Interval:

```
> library(PropCIs)
> add4ci(49,129,conf.level=0.95)

data:

95 percent confidence interval:
 0.3008239 0.4660934
sample estimates:
[1] 0.3834586

> scoreci(49,129,conf.level=0.95)

data:

95 percent confidence interval:
 0.3007 0.4659
```

Most likely because our sample proportion is not extremely high or extremely low, the alternative confidence interval methods are a *little* smaller, bounding the possibilities for our true population proportion just a little tighter. That's OK.

Check Results in R

We can run this test in R to check our work. However, `prop.test` doesn't use the same equations we used to calculate our test statistic z. Instead, `prop.test` computes a *chi-square* test statistic with the Yates continuity correction, which should be a little more exact. Find out more at https://en.wikipedia.org/wiki/Yates%27s_correction_for_continuity.

We'll double check in two ways: using `z.test` (a function you can source from GitHub, that performs the same calculations that you did analytically) and also using `prop.test`. First, obtain the code for the `z.test` function:

```
source("https://raw.githubusercontent.com/NicoleRadziwill/R-
Functions/master/ztest.R")
```

```
> z.test(49,129,alternative="greater",p=0.45)
$estimate
[1] 0.379845

$ts.z
[1] -1.601644

$p.val
[1] 0.9453829

$cint
[1] 0.2939949 0.4656951
```

The test statistic, P-Value, and confidence interval bounds are the same as what we calculated analytically. Finally, let's try the same thing with `prop.test`:

```
> prop.test(49,129,alternative="greater",p=0.45)

        1-sample proportions test with continuity correction

data:  49 out of 129, null probability 0.45
X-squared = 2.2896, df = 1, p-value = 0.9349
alternative hypothesis: true p is greater than 0.45
95 percent confidence interval:
0.309047 1.000000
```

```
sample estimates:
      p
0.379845
```

The p-value is similar to the one we got when we computed our test statistic z, and the conclusion (that we should fail to reject) the null hypothesis remains the same. We can also very easily test any of the *other* possible null hypotheses, for example:

H_0: $p = 0.45$
H_a: $p < 0.45$

```
> prop.test(49,129,alternative="less",p=0.45)


        1-sample proportions test with continuity correction

data:   49 out of 129, null probability 0.45
X-squared = 2.2896, df = 1, p-value = 0.06512
alternative hypothesis: true p is less than 0.45
95 percent confidence interval:
0.0000000 0.4558487
sample estimates:
      p
0.379845
```

The results indicate that we should fail to reject the null hypothesis, but we would be right on the edge of the decision boundary had we selected a level of significance of 0.05 – so *some* effect might be in play here. Using R, we can quickly run the same tests for the SNAP_R case, and compute confidence intervals. Notice that the confidence intervals prepared in prop.test only compute correctly when you leave off the alternative hypothesis you are testing against.

```
> prop.test(275,819,alternative="greater",p=0.45)


        1-sample proportions test with continuity correction

data:   275 out of 819, null probability 0.45
X-squared = 42.714, df = 1, p-value = 1   # Fail to Reject!
alternative hypothesis: true p is greater than 0.45
95 percent confidence interval:
0.3086155 1.0000000
sample estimates:
      p
0.3357753
```

```
> prop.test(275,819,alternative="less",p=0.45)

        1-sample proportions test with continuity correction

data:  275 out of 819, null probability 0.45
X-squared = 42.714, df = 1, p-value = 3.167e-11 # Reject!
alternative hypothesis: true p is less than 0.45
95 percent confidence interval:
0.0000000 0.3640409
sample estimates:
       p
0.3357753


> prop.test(275,819,p=0.45)

        1-sample proportions test with continuity correction

data:  275 out of 819, null probability 0.45
X-squared = 42.714, df = 1, p-value = 6.335e-11 # Reject the two-tailed case!
alternative hypothesis: true p is not equal to 0.45
95 percent confidence interval:
0.3036717 0.3694412
sample estimates:
       p
0.3357753
```

The "Add 4" confidence interval and the Wilson score are nearly identical for the SNAP_R case:

```
> add4ci(275,819,conf.level=0.95)

data:
95 percent confidence interval:
0.3042897 0.3688573
sample estimates:
[1] 0.3365735

> scoreci(275,819,conf.level=0.95)

data:
95 percent confidence interval:
0.3043 0.3688
```

Consequently, **we are 95% confident that the true proportion of victims that succumb to SNAP_R is between 30.4% and 36.9%.** This is definitely lower than the magic proportion of 45%.

Two Proportion z-test: Public Opinion on Healthcare Reform

A poll on March 23rd, 2017 reported that 228 out of 406 American women were opposed to the healthcare reform bill, while 291 out of 580 American men were. **Do a greater proportion of women oppose the bill?**

Women (Group 1)	Men (Group 2)
n = 406 x = 228 p-hat = x/n = 228/406 = 0.562 q-hat = 1 - 0.562 = 0.438	n = 580 x = 297 p-hat = x/n = 297/580 = 0.502 q-hat = 1 - 0.502 = 0.498

Step 0: Check Assumptions

- **Random sample** - We were told that this is a random sample. ✔
- **Observations are independent** - Although there may be a chance that one survey respondent encouraged a friend to *think the same way as them*, or maybe even to think differently, this is unlikely especially if the polling firm did a good job collecting a random and representative sample. The observations appear independent. ✔
- **Sample is small enough** - Are our samples of 406 and 580 people less than 10% of the population of all Americans? Most certainly, yes. ✔
- **Sample is large enough** - For both groups, (n * p-hat) and (n * q-hat) have to be greater than 10. We can affirm that approximately half of 406, and approximately half of 580, will definitely be greater than 10. ✔
- **Independent Groups** - The groups do not overlap and it is unlikely that the results from one group influenced the results from the other group. ✔

Women (Group 1)	Men (Group 2)
n*p-hat = 406 * 0.562 = 228.2 n*q-hat = 406 * 0.438 = 177.83	n*p-hat = 580 * 0.502 = 291.16 n*q-hat = 580 * 0.498 = 288.84

Step 1: Set Null (H₀) & Alternative (Hₐ) Hypotheses:

H₀: **$p_1 - p_2 = p_0$** p_0 is the expected difference between proportions. Set $p_0 = 0$

Hₐ: **$p_1 - p_2 > p_0$**   Then, PICK ONE version from the alternatives. We want to
$p_1 - p_2 < p_0$ know if a greater proportion of women oppose the bill, so we pick
$p_1 - p_2 \neq p_0$ top ("greater than") option.

Step 2: Set α, the Level of Significance:

An **α of 0.05** means that **1 out of every 20 times** we collect data to run this test, we accept that we will *reject the null hypothesis* when that's the wrong thing to do. Is this level of significance OK? There are three things we have to consider: **cost** of getting new data, the **risk** of making an incorrect decision based on this test, and the **ethical considerations** associated with someone else using our results to make *their* decisions.

- First, does it cost a lot to get more data? Not really, but putting together sound sampling strategies does take time and effort.
- Second, what decision will I make based on this test? I could be gathering data for a public or government source, or maybe I'm going to share my conclusions with a media outlet. Both possibilities mean that lots of people will be exposed to my analysis.
- Finally, will anyone else be using my data or analysis to make *their* decisions? That's definitely a possibility.

As a result, let's go with an **α of 0.01.** I'd rather only be wrong 1 out of every 100 samples I collect. Those stakes are somewhat high.

Step 3: Calculate Test Statistic (T.S.)

This is a two-proportion z-test, so the test statistic we want to compute is a **z.** (This also means we will use the normal distribution when we draw our picture). For the standard error, we find p by adding up all the successes ($x_1 + x_2$) and dividing by the total number of observations ($n_1 + n_2$). Because p = (228 + 297) / (406 + 580) = 0.532, that means q = 1 - p = 0.468. Now we have all the numbers we need to find the test statistic z:

$$z = \frac{\hat{p}_1 - \hat{p}_2 - p_0}{SE(\hat{p}_1 - \hat{p}_2)} = \frac{\hat{p}_1 - \hat{p}_2 - p_0}{\sqrt{pq\left(\frac{1}{n_1} + \frac{1}{n_2}\right)}}$$

$$z = \frac{0.562 - 0.502}{\sqrt{(0.532 \times 0.468)\left(\frac{1}{406} + \frac{1}{580}\right)}} = \frac{0.06}{0.032} = 1.875$$

Step 4: Draw a Picture

The value of z that we calculated is approximately z=1.875. This is quite a bit to the right of the mean in the distribution that we're using to represent our null hypothesis. By making an arrow out of the sign in our alternative hypothesis, we know to shade the area to the right of z=1.875. The picture shows the area we will be trying to find in Step 5, which is just a tiny bit bigger than 2.5% (that's the area to the right of z=+2, from our 68-95-99.7 Rule).

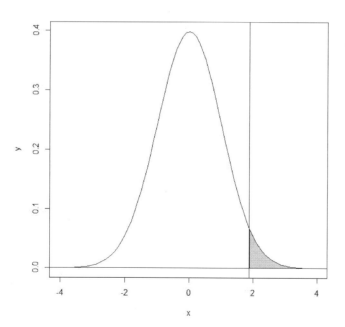

Here's the code that produced this plot:

```
x <- seq(-4,4,0.1)
y <- dnorm(x)
plot(x,y,type="l")
abline(h=0)
abline(v=1.875)


> which(x=="1.9")   # it's the closest one
[1]  60


polygon(c(x[60:81],rev(x[60:81])), c(rep(0,22),rev(y[60:81])), col="lightgray")
```

Step 5: Calculate P-Value

From Step 4, we estimated that the total area (our P-value) will be slightly bigger than 2.5%. Now let's find out exactly how large the shaded area is. Since R looks up the area of the left tail, we have to subtract the left tail area from 1:

```
> 1-pnorm(1.875)
[1]  0.03039636
```

Just as we expected, the area is 3%... slightly larger than 2.5%.

Step 6: Draw Conclusion

Is the P-Value < α? If so, reject the null hypothesis (H₀).

Is 0.03 < 0.01? **No, it is not.** We **fail to reject** the null hypothesis (H₀) that the proportion of women who oppose healthcare reform is greater than the proportion of men who oppose it. Note that if we had used a less stringent alpha of 0.05, we *would* have rejected the null hypothesis, and concluded that a greater proportion of women opposed the 2017 healthcare reform effort.

Step 7: Compute Confidence Interval & Double Check in R

Always start with the general form of the confidence interval (that is, *write these words*):

CI: Estimate ± Margin of Error

Next, replace those words with the values you'll need to look up or calculate:

CI: (Difference between Sample Proportions) ± z* (Standard Error of the Difference)

The left-hand side, with the difference between proportions, is just the numerator from our calculation of the test statistic z. Next, we find the Standard Error of the proportion (the denominator from when we calculated our test statistic z) which is 0.032. Finally, we plug in the values from our sample data, using z* = 1.96 (which hopefully you've memorized as one of the three most commonly used critical z's for confidence intervals - the one that corresponds to a CI of 95%):

CI: 0.06 ± (1.96 x 0.032)

After computing the lower and upper bounds, we can say **we are 95% confident that the true difference between proportions is between -0.3% and 12.3%.** So there's a tiny chance that the true difference between proportions is zero.

We can run this test in R to check our work. However, `prop.test` doesn't use the same equations we used to calculate our test statistic z. Instead, `prop.test` computes a *chi-square* test statistic with the Yates continuity correction, which should be a little more exact. Find out more at https://en.wikipedia.org/wiki/Yates%27s_correction_for_continuity. We'll double check in two ways: using `z2.test` (a function you can source from GitHub, that performs the same calculations that you did analytically) and also using `prop.test`. First, obtain the code for the `z2.test` function:

```
source("https://raw.githubusercontent.com/NicoleRadziwill/R-
Functions/master/z2test.R")
```

The z2.test function takes the number of successes (`x1` and `x2`) and the total number of opportunities (`n1` and `n2`) in any order, as long as they are labeled:

```
> z2.test(x1=228,x2=291,n1=406,n2=580 ,alternative="greater")
$estimate
[1] 0.05985222

$ts.z
[1] 1.85248

$p.val
[1] 0.03197844
```

```
$cint
[1] -0.001681888  0.121386322
```

The test statistic, P-Value, and confidence interval bounds are very nearly the same as what we calculated analytically. Finally, you can see similar results with `prop.test`:

```
> prop.test(c(228,291),c(406,580))


        2-sample test for equality of proportions with continuity correction

data:  c(228, 291) out of c(406, 580)
X-squared = 3.1958, df = 1, p-value = 0.07383
alternative hypothesis: two.sided
95 percent confidence interval:
-0.0053709  0.1250753
sample estimates:
  prop 1    prop 2
0.5615764 0.5017241
```

We draw our conclusion by looking at the p-value. Is 0.07 < 0.01? No, not at all. We fail to reject the null hypothesis, which tells us that women and men opposed healthcare reform in approximately equal proportions. We can double check the calculation of our confidence interval by dropping the specification of the alternative hypothesis:

```
> prop.test(c(228,291),c(406,580))


        2-sample test for equality of proportions with continuity correction

data:  c(228, 291) out of c(406, 580)
X-squared = 3.1958, df = 1, p-value = 0.07383
alternative hypothesis: two.sided
95 percent confidence interval:
-0.0053709  0.1250753
sample estimates:
  prop 1    prop 2
0.5615764 0.5017241
```

Just like we calculated, we are 95% confident that the true difference is between -0.5% and 12.5%, very similar to what we calculated earlier. If we wanted a more exact confidence interval, we could try using the `PropCIs` or `pairwiseCI` packages, although with p's and q's near the 50% mark, we should not expect much improvement - alternative methods tend to work better when the proportions are closer to 0% or 100%.

Two Proportion z-test: Marijuana Legalization

An online poll on January 10, 2017 reported that 97 out of 120 people in Virginia between the ages of 18 and 29 believe marijuana should be legal, while 84 out of 111 who are 30 and over held this belief. **Is there a difference between the proportion of young people who favor marijuana legalization as compared to people who are older?**

Age 18-29 (Group 1)	Age 30+ (Group 2)
n = 120 x = 97 p-hat = x/n = 97/120 = 0.808 q-hat = 1 - 0.808 = 0.202	n = 111 x = 84 p-hat = x/n = 84/111 = 0.757 q-hat = 1 - 0.757 = 0.243

Step 0: Check Assumptions

- **Random sample** - We don't know for sure, but we'll assume that this is a random sample. Online surveys sometimes have serious problems with bias, but we don't have any way to find out details about the sampling. We'll take the results with a grain of salt. ☑
- **Observations are independent** - Although there may be a chance that one survey respondent encouraged a friend to *think similarly or differently*, this is unlikely especially if the people conducting the survey did a good job with their sampling. The observations appear independent. ☑
- **Sample is small enough** - Are our samples of 120 and 111 people less than 10% of the population of Virginia? Most certainly, yes. ☑
- **Sample is large enough** - For both groups, (n * p-hat) and (n * q-hat) have to be greater than 10. We can affirm that 20% of 120 and 24% of 111 will definitely be greater than 10. ☑
- **Independent Groups** - The groups do not overlap and it is unlikely that the results from one group influenced the results from the other group. ☑

Younger (Group 1)	Older (Group 2)
n*p-hat = 120 * 0.808 = 96.96 n*q-hat = 120 * 0.202 = 24.24	n*p-hat = 111 * 0.757 = 84.03 n*q-hat = 111 * 0.243 = 26.97

Step 1: Set Null (H₀) & Alternative (Hₐ) Hypotheses

H₀: **p₁ - p₂ = p₀**   p₀ is the expected difference between proportions. Set p₀ = 0

Hₐ: p₁ - p₂ > p₀   Then, PICK ONE version from the alternatives. We don't care
           p₁ - p₂ < p₀   which proportion is bigger, we just want to know if there's a
           p₁ - p₂ ≠ p₀   difference. So we pick the bottom (third) option.

Step 2: Set α, the Level of Significance:

An **α of 0.05** means that **1 out of every 20 times** we collect data to run this test, we accept that we will *reject the null hypothesis* when that's the wrong thing to do. Is this level of significance OK? There are three things we have to consider: **cost** of getting new data, the **risk** of making an incorrect decision based on this test, and the **ethical considerations** associated with someone else using our results to make *their* decisions.

- First, does it cost a lot to get more data? No.
- Second, what decision will I make based on this test? Nothing critical. I just want to know if there's a difference between the opinions of these two age groups.
- Finally, will anyone else be using my data or analysis to make *their* decisions? Definitely not.

As a result, let's go with an **α of 0.05.** The stakes are not high.

Step 3: Calculate Test Statistic (T.S.)

This is a two-proportion z-test, so the test statistic we want to compute is a **z.** (This also means we will use the normal distribution when we draw our picture). For the standard error, we find p by adding up all the successes ($x_1 + x_2$) and dividing by the total number of observations ($n_1 + n_2$). Because p = (97 + 84) / (120 + 111) = 0.784, that means q = 1 - p = 0.216. Now we have all the numbers we need to find the test statistic z:

$$z = \frac{\hat{p}_1 - \hat{p}_2 - p_0}{SE(\hat{p}_1 - \hat{p}_2)} = \frac{\hat{p}_1 - \hat{p}_2 - p_0}{\sqrt{pq\left(\frac{1}{n_1} + \frac{1}{n_2}\right)}}$$

$$z = \frac{0.808 - 0.757}{\sqrt{(0.784 \; x \; 0.216)\left(\frac{1}{120} + \frac{1}{111}\right)}} = \frac{0.051}{0.054} = 0.944$$

Step 4: Draw a Picture

The value of z that we calculated is approximately z=0.944. This is quite a bit to the right of the mean in the distribution that we're using to represent our null hypothesis. We can't make an arrow out of the sign in our alternative hypothesis, so we know to shade the area to the right of z=0.944 *and* to the left of z=-0.944. The picture shows the area we will be trying to find in Step 5, which will be approximately 32% (that's the area outside z=-1 and z=+1, from our 68-95-99.7 Rule, or 100% - 68% = 32%).

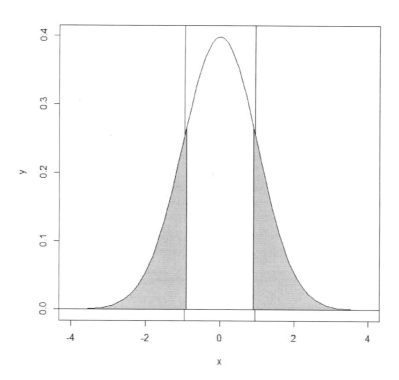

Here's the code that produced that plot:

```
x <- seq(-4,4,0.1)
y <- dnorm(x)
plot(x,y,type="l")
abline(h=0)
abline(v=0.944)
abline(v=-0.944)


> which(x=="0.9")   # these are the closest points on our plot to z
[1] 50
> which(x=="-0.9")
[1] 32


polygon(c(x[1:32],rev(x[1:32])), c(rep(0,32),rev(y[1:32])), col="lightgray")
polygon(c(x[50:81],rev(x[50:81])), c(rep(0,32),rev(y[50:81])), col="lightgray")
```

Step 5: Calculate P-Value

From Step 4, we estimated that the total area (our P-value) will be huge, around 32%. Now let's find out exactly how large the shaded area is. Since R looks up the area of the left tail, we have to find the left tail area and then multiply it by 2:

```
> 2 * pnorm(-0.944)
[1] 0.3451696
```

Just as we expected, the area is 34.5%... slightly larger than our estimate of 32%.

Step 6: Draw Conclusion

Is the P-Value < α? If so, reject the null hypothesis (H$_0$).

Is 0.345 < 0.01? **No, it is not.** We **fail to reject** the null hypothesis (H$_0$) that the proportion of young people who support legalization is different than the proportion of older people who support it.

Step 7: Compute Confidence Interval & Double Check in R

You can compare this conclusion to the confidence interval. Always start with the general form of the confidence interval (that is, *write these words*):

CI: Estimate ± Margin of Error

Next, replace those words with the values you'll need to look up or calculate:

CI: (Difference between Sample Proportions) ± z* (Standard Error of the Difference)

The left-hand side, with the difference between proportions, is just the numerator from our calculation of the test statistic z of 0.051. Next, we look up the Standard Error of the proportion (the denominator from when we calculated our test statistic z) which is 0.054. Finally, we plug in the values from our sample data, using z* = 1.96 (which hopefully you've memorized as one of the three most commonly used critical z's for confidence intervals - the one that corresponds to a CI of 95%):

CI: 0.051 ± (1.96 x 0.054)

After computing the lower and upper bounds, we can say **we are 95% confident that the true difference between proportions is between -5.4% and 15.6%.** So there's definitely a chance that the true difference between proportions is zero.

We can run this test in R to check our work. However, `prop.test` doesn't use the same equations we used to calculate our test statistic z. Instead, `prop.test` computes a *chi-square* test statistic with the Yates continuity correction, which should be a little more exact. Find out more at https://en.wikipedia.org/wiki/Yates%27s_correction_for_continuity.

We'll double check in two ways: using `z2.test` (a function you can source from GitHub, that performs the same calculations that you did analytically) and also using `prop.test`. First, obtain the code for the `z2.test` function:

```
source("https://raw.githubusercontent.com/NicoleRadziwill/R-
Functions/master/z2test.R")
```

The `z2.test` function takes the number of successes (`x1` and `x2`) and the total number of opportunities (`n1` and `n2`) in any order, as long as they are labeled. You can also provide this function with any `conf.level` (e.g. 0.99 for a 99% CI) and `alternative="greater"` or `alternative="less"`:

```
> z2.test(x1=97,n1=120,x2=84,n2=111)
```

```
$estimate
[1] 0.05157658

$ts.z
[1] 0.9510127

$p.val
[1] 0.3415979

$cint
[1] -0.04832008  0.15147323
```

The values for test statistic, P-Value, and confidence interval bounds are very nearly what we calculated analytically.

```
> prop.test(c(97,84),c(120,111))


        2-sample test for equality of proportions with continuity correction

data:  c(97, 84) out of c(120, 111)
X-squared = 0.62588, df = 1, p-value = 0.4289
alternative hypothesis: two.sided
95 percent confidence interval:
 -0.0635376  0.1666908
sample estimates:
   prop 1    prop 2
0.8083333 0.7567568
```

Although the P-Value is higher using the Chi-square test, the conclusion remains the same. We draw our conclusion by looking at the p-value. Is 0.4289 < 0.05? No, not at all. We fail to reject the null hypothesis, which tells us that there is no difference between the proportions. Because we did the two-tailed test (with the not equal sign in the alternative hypothesis) we can trust the calculations of the confidence interval from this output as well. Using the corrections employed by R, we are 95% confident that the true difference in proportions is between -6.4% and 16.6% - numbers very close to what we calculated analytically.

Two proportion z-test: SNAP_R Phishing Utility vs. Humans

Find out more about SNAP_R at https://www.blackhat.com/docs/us-16/materials/us-16-Seymour-Tully-Weaponizing-Data-Science-For-Social-Engineering-Automated-E2E-Spear-Phishing-On-Twitter.pdf

SNAP_R is a program written to automate the process of "spear phishing" - that is, contacting an individual online while masquerading as a "trusted source" and convincing him or her to divulge sensitive personal (or business) information. I found out about this tool watching a video from DEFCON 24, an annual hacker's conference held in Las Vegas. They provided some observations about how many times their victims clicked malicious links based on whether humans or SNAP_R were doing the phishing. We were told that **the hackers running this test convinced 275 people out of 819 to click through, compared to 49 out of 129 when a human was doing the phishing.** With this data, we can answer three research questions:

1. **Do humans get greater than 45% click-through?**
2. **Does SNAP_R get greater than 45% click-through?** (That is, does this new software effectively steal victims' personal information?)
3. **Does SNAP_R snag a different percentage of victims than human phishers?**

We answered the first two of these questions using the one proportion z-test in a previous chapter. We will do #3 analytically and in R using the two-proportion z-test. Here's our data:

Human Phisher	SNAP_R Phisher
n = 129 x = 49	n = 819 x = 275
p-hat = x/n = 49/129 = 0.38 q-hat = 1 - 0.380 = 0.62	p-hat = x/n = 275/819 = 0.336 q-hat = 1 - 0.336 = 0.664

Step 0: Check Assumptions

- **Random sample** - We are told that this is a random sample. ✔
- **Observations are independent** - Although there may be a chance that one victim encouraged a friend to *also click on the phishing link*, this is unlikely. The observations appear independent. ✔

- **Sample is small enough** - Are our samples of 129 and 819 people less than 10% of the size of the entire population of phishing victims? Unfortunately, yes. ✔
- **Sample is large enough** - The probability of "success" is the probability of getting hacked, so the calculations below affirm that we have a large enough sample... all values > 10. ✔

Human Phisher	SNAP_R Phisher
n*p-hat = 129 * 0.38 = 49 n*q-hat = 129 * 0.62 = 80	n*p-hat = 819 * 0.336 = 275.2 n*q-hat = 819 * 0.664 = 543.8

Step 1: Set Null (H$_o$) & Alternative (H$_a$) Hypotheses:

H$_0$: $p_{SNAP} - p_{HUMAN} = p_0$ We will set p$_0$ = 0 and assume that there is no difference.

H$_a$: $p_{SNAP} - p_{HUMAN} > p_0$

$p_{SNAP} - p_{HUMAN} < p_0$ We pick the "different than" option because we want to know if the proportions of victims are the same, or not.

$p_{SNAP} - p_{HUMAN} \neq p_0$

Step 2: Set α, the Level of Significance:

An **α of 0.05** means that **1 out of every 20 times** we collect data to run this test, we accept that we will *reject the null hypothesis* when that's the wrong thing to do. Is this level of significance OK? There are three things we have to consider: **cost** of getting new data, the **risk** of making an incorrect decision based on this test, and the **ethical considerations** associated with someone else using our results to make *their* decisions.

- First, does it cost a lot to get more data? Sort of. Phishing is labor intensive.
- Second, what decision will I make based on this test? I could be deciding whether to use SNAP_R for my nefarious purposes, or maybe I'm trying to decide whether to commit new resources (time, money, and labor) to the development project. Both decisions are substantial.
- Finally, will anyone else be using my data or analysis to make *their* decisions? That's definitely a possibility.

As a result, let's go with an **α of 0.01.** I'd rather only be wrong 1 out of every 100 samples I collect. Those stakes are somewhat high.

Step 3: Calculate Test Statistic (T.S.)

This is a two-proportion z-test, so the test statistic we want to compute is a **z.** (This also means we will use the normal distribution). For the standard error, we use the p and q determined by adding up all the successes (49 + 275) and dividing them by all the opportunities (129 + 819). As a result, p (no hat) will be 0.341 and q will be 1-0.341 = 0.659. Group 1 are the human phishers, and Group 2 is SNAP_R:

$$z = \frac{\hat{p}_1 - \hat{p}_2 - p_0}{SE(\hat{p}_1 - \hat{p}_2)} = \frac{\hat{p}_1 - \hat{p}_2 - p_0}{\sqrt{pq\left(\frac{1}{n_1} + \frac{1}{n_2}\right)}}$$

$$z = \frac{0.336 - 0.380)}{\sqrt{0.341 \ x \ 0.659 \left(\frac{1}{129} + \frac{1}{819}\right)}} = 0.980$$

Step 4: Draw a Picture

Since our alternative hypothesis has the "not equal" sign in it, we have to find the total area of the tail to the left of z=-0.98 *plus* the area of the tail to the right of z=+0.98. We can get a fairly good estimate of the area in the tails using the 68-95-99.7 Rule since z is so close to 1, so we don't need to draw a picture. The estimated area is 100%-68% = 32%.

Step 5: Calculate P-Value

From Step 4, we estimated that the total area (our P-value) will be nearly 100%. Now let's find out exactly how large the shaded area is:

```
> 2 * pnorm(-0.98)
[1] 0.3270861
```

As expected, 32.7% of the area is in these two tails.

Step 6: Draw Conclusion

Is the P-Value < α? If so, reject the null hypothesis (H₀).

Is 0.964 < 0.01? **No, it is not.** We **fail to reject** the null hypothesis (H₀) that the proportion of victims is different whether we used SNAP_R or humans for phishing. That's a good thing! It suggests that the software is already obtaining sensitive information with *at least* the level of success as the humans. Because software is less expensive than humans, we no longer need to retain our human phishermen: we can release as many SNAP_R agents as we like, and proceed to wreak havoc on humanity. (See how some statistical decisions can be importance?")

Disclaimer: I don't actually mean that. I most certainly don't advocate cybercrime.

Step 7: Compute Confidence Interval & Double Check in R

Always start with the general form of the confidence interval (that is, *write these words*):

CI: Estimate ± Margin of Error

Next, replace those words with the values you'll need to look up or calculate:

CI: (Difference between Sample Proportions) ± z* (Standard Error of the Difference)

$$CI : (\hat{p}_1 - \hat{p}_2) \pm z^* SE(\hat{p}_1 - \hat{p}_2)$$

$$CI : (\hat{p}_1 - \hat{p}_2) \pm z^* \sqrt{\left(\frac{\hat{p}_1 \hat{q}_1}{n_1} + \frac{\hat{p}_2 \hat{q}_2}{n_2} \right)}$$

First we compute the Standard Error of the difference (the values inside the square root):

```
> sqrt( ((.38*.62)/129)   + ((.336*.664)/819)   )
[1] 0.0458123
```

Finally, we plug in the values from our sample data, using z* = 1.96 (which hopefully you've memorized as one of the three most commonly used critical z's for confidence intervals):

CI: 0.044 ± (1.96 x 0.046)

After computing the lower and upper bounds, we can say **we are 95% confident that the true difference in proportions of victims who have succumbed to phishing attempts by humans versus SNAP_R is between -4.6% and 13.4%.** Because zero is one of the possibilities in our confidence interval, this supports our decision earlier where we failed to reject the null. There is no evidence that the phishing success rates are different.

We can run this test in R to check our work. However, `prop.test` doesn't use the same equations we used to calculate our test statistic z. Instead, `prop.test` computes a *chi-square* test statistic with the Yates continuity correction, which should be a little more exact. Find out more at https://en.wikipedia.org/wiki/Yates%27s_correction_for_continuity. We'll double check in two ways: using `z2.test` (a function you can source from GitHub, that performs the same calculations that you did analytically) and also using `prop.test`. First, obtain the code for the `z2.test` function:

```
source("https://raw.githubusercontent.com/NicoleRadziwill/R-
Functions/master/z2test.R")
```

The `z2.test` function takes the number of successes (`x1` and `x2`) and the total number of opportunities (`n1` and `n2`) in any order, as long as they are labeled. You can also provide this function with any `conf.level` (e.g. 0.99 for a 99% CI) and `alternative="greater"` or `alternative="less"`:

```
> z2.test(x1=49,n1=129,x2=275,n2=819)
$estimate
[1] 0.04406963

$ts.z
[1] 0.9808792

$p.val
[1] 0.3266523

$cint
[1] -0.04532537  0.13346462
```

The test statistic, P-Value, and confidence interval bounds agree with our analytical soltuions. Now let's try the prop.test approach:

```
> my.props <- cbind(c(49,275),c(129,819))
> prop.test(my.props)

        2-sample test for equality of proportions with continuity correction

data:  my.props
```

```
X-squared = 0.34368, df = 1, p-value = 0.5577
alternative hypothesis: two.sided
95 percent confidence interval:
-0.04982801  0.09764758
sample estimates:
  prop 1     prop 2
0.2752809 0.2513711
```

The P-Value is a little higher, but the results indicate that we should fail to reject the null hypothesis that the proportions are the same, which corroborates our earlier conclusion. (Don't be alarmed that the p-value is so much different than the one we calculated... remember, R uses a chi-square approach in prop.test, so the test statistic is different.)

Let's double check the confidence interval calculations using functions in the PropCIs package, which tend to be more accurate than the ones we computed analytically. Looks like it's also in agreement with our earlier calculations:

```
> wald2ci(49,129,275,819,conf.level=0.95,adjust=TRUE)

data:

95 percent confidence interval:
 -0.04374101  0.13474899
sample estimates:
[1] 0.04550399
```

Chi-Square Test of Independence: Packaging Design

A marketing firm is exploring different possibilities for product configurations and packaging for a vitamin-packed juice beverage. In this test, for two packaging designs that can be offered to the customer at the same price point, they want to know: **Is preferred packaging related to income level?** They suspect that the eco-friendly option is more desired by upper middle-class buyers, but want to know for sure.

	Low	Middle	Upper Middle
Plastic	47	51	33
Eco-Friendly	43	63	76

Step 0: Check Assumptions

- **Random sample** - Although we don't know what sampling strategy was used, because it's being done by a marketing firm, we will assume that the sample is random. ✔
- **Observations are independent** - We don't know for sure, but it seems reasonable that one person's answer will not have affected another person's answer, so observations are independent. ✔
- **Sample is small enough** - Is our sample of n=313 customers less than 10% of the size of the entire population of customers? Hopefully, yes... we want more than 3000 total potential customers. ✔
- **At least 5 (or 10) counts per cell** - There are well over the minimum observations in each cell. ✔

Step 1: Set Null (H₀) & Alternative (Hₐ) Hypotheses:

For the Chi-square test of independence, just plug in the names of your two categorical variables to the null and alternative hypotheses:

H_0: Packaging type and income level are independent.
H_a: Packaging type and income level are *not* independent.

If we reject the null in favor of the alternative, that means something *interesting* is going on: one or more of the income levels may prefer one of the two types of packaging, because the observations are not distributed in the same way they would be if there was no relationship.

Step 2: Set α, the Level of Significance:

An **α of 0.05** means that **1 out of every 20 times** we collect data to run this test, we accept that we will *reject the null hypothesis* when that's the wrong answer. Is this OK? There are three things we have to consider: **cost** of getting new data, the **risk** of making an incorrect decision based on this test, and the **ethical considerations** associated with someone else using our results to make *their* decisions.

- First, does it cost a lot to get more data? Not really.
- Second, what decision will I make based on this test? If I work for the marketing company, and my choice of packaging depends (in part) on the results of this test, then there's a lot of stake. Not only will this decision influence who I partner with to manufacture the packaging materials, but my customers will also see this packaging until we change it the next time around.
- Finally, will anyone else be using my data or analysis to make *their* decisions? Probably yes. We know that all quantitative analysis is shared among employees and managers at this marketing company, so there's always a chance.

As a result, let's instead choose an **α of 0.01,** meaning that **1 out of every 100 times** we run this test, we will *reject the null hypothesis* when that's the wrong thing to do. If we draw this conclusion, we're going to invest time, effort, and maybe money chasing a problem that doesn't exist. But by choosing this value for our level of significance, we're establishing a basis for acceptable risk: if we draw an incorrect conclusion one time we run this test every 100, that's OK.

Step 3: Calculate Test Statistic (T.S.)

This is a Chi-square test of independence, so our test statistic is a χ^2:

$$\chi^2 = \sum_{cells} \frac{(Observed - Expected)^2}{Expected}$$

We will find the value for χ^2 by using R as a calculator. First, we construct the contingency table and tack on the marginal distributions as `col.totals` and `row.totals`:

```
> plastic <- c(47,51,33)
> eco <- c(43,63,76)
> simple.ct <- rbind(plastic,eco)   # Contingency table without row and column totals
> col.totals <- plastic+eco
> row.totals <- c(sum(plastic),sum(eco),sum(col.totals))
> full.ct <- rbind(plastic,eco,col.totals)
> full.ct <- cbind(full.ct,row.totals)
> full.ct
                        row.totals
plastic     47  51  33       131
eco         43  63  76       182
col.totals  90 114 109       313
```

We will find the value for χ^2 by using the formula above. I'm going to create new variables called `expected` and `observed` so that it's easier to see how we're calculating the value of the test statistic. The expected values for each cell are found by multiplying the *row total for that cell* by the *column total for that cell*, and then dividing by the *total total* that's in the bottom right hand corner of the full contingency table.

```
> expected <- c( ((131*90)/313), ((131*114)/313), ((131*109)/313),
((182*90)/313), ((182*114)/313), ((182*109)/313) )
> observed <- c( 47, 51, 33, 43, 63, 76 )
> chi.sqrd <- sum(  ((observed-expected)^2)/expected  )
> chi.sqrd
[1] 10.36964
```

Step 4: Draw a Picture

The value of χ^2 that we calculated is approximately $\chi^2=10.36$. Before we draw the picture, we need to know the degrees of freedom which we calculate using `df=(rows-1)(cols-1)`. Since we have 2 rows and 3 columns, df = 1 x 2 = 2. The area in the right tail will be very, very tiny.

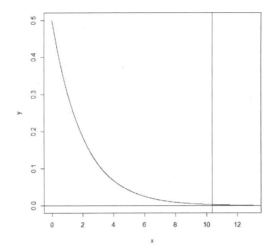

Here is the code that produced that plot:

```
> x <- seq(0,13,0.01)
> y <- dchisq(x, df=2)
> plot(x,y,type="1")
> abline(v=+10.36)
> abline(h=0)
> which(x=="0.96")
[1] 97
> which(x=="10.36")
[1] 1037
> length(x)
[1] 1301
> 1301-1037+1
[1] 265
> polygon(c(x[1037:1301],rev(x[1037:1301])), c(rep(0,265),rev(y[1037:1301])),
col="lightgray")
```

This is so far to the right on our picture of the Chi-square distribution that we know the area in the tail, the p-value, will be about zero.

Step 5: Calculate P-Value

From Step 4, we estimated that the total shaded area (our P-value) will be about zero. Now let's find out exactly how large the shaded area is. Since `pchisq` finds the area to the left, we have to subtract from 1 to get the area to the right:

```
> 1-pchisq(10.36,df=2)
[1] 0.005628006
```

The area to the right of our calculated test statistic is approximately half a percent.

Step 6: Draw Conclusion

Is the P-Value < α? If so, reject the null hypothesis (H₀).

Is 0.00562 < 0.01? **Yes it is.** We **reject** the null hypothesis (H₀) that income level and packaging preference are independent. *There is indeed some relationship* and we probably want to explore it more.

Step 7: Construct a Confidence Interval & Double Check in R

There is no confidence interval for this test, however, you can create confidence intervals on one proportion (e.g. the % of preferring eco-friendly packaging) or the difference between proportions e.g. (% of observations in each income category that prefer each of the packaging types). We can, though, run the test in R to see if we've calculated our test statistic and p-value correctly. We call chisq.test on the contingency table that contains *just* the raw data (without the totals in the margins), using correct=FALSE. (Although it looks like we're telling R to get the wrong answer, what we're *actually* asking is that Yates' continuity correction is not applied.) Notice that the test statistic, the degrees of freedom, and the P-value are exactly what we calculated.

```
> chisq.test(simple.ct, correct=FALSE)

        Pearson's Chi-squared test

data:  simple.ct
X-squared = 10.37, df = 2, p-value = 0.005601
```

Chi-Square Test of Independence: Flavor Preference

A marketing firm is exploring different possibilities for product configurations and packaging for a vitamin-packed juice beverage. In this test, they want to explore differences in flavor preference: **Does preferred flavor depend on age group?** They have a feeling that only the older people like the lemon flavor, but want to know for sure.

	Under 13	13-20	21-30	31-40
Lemon	26	30	31	34
Berry	34	31	29	30
Watermelon	31	30	33	34

Step 0: Check Assumptions

- **Random sample** - Although we don't know what sampling strategy was used, because it's being done by a marketing firm, we will assume that the sample is random. ☑
- **Observations are independent** - We don't know for sure, but it seems reasonable that one person's answer will not have affected another person's answer, so observations are independent. ☑
- **Sample is small enough** - Is our sample of n=373 customers less than 10% of the size of the entire population of customers? Hopefully, yes... we want more than 3700 total potential customers. ☑
- **At least 5 (or 10) counts per cell** - There are well over the minimum observations in each cell. ☑

Step 1: Set Null (H₀) & Alternative (Hₐ) Hypotheses:

For the Chi-square test of independence, just plug in the names of your two categorical variables to the null and alternative hypotheses:

H₀: Preferred flavor and age group are independent.
Hₐ: Preferred flavor and age group are *not* independent.

If we reject the null in favor of the alternative, that means something *interesting* is going on: one or more of the age groups may prefer one of the three flavors, because the observations are not distributed in the same way they would be if there was no relationship.

Step 2: Set α, the Level of Significance:

An **α of 0.05** means that **1 out of every 20 times** we collect data to run this test, we accept that we will *reject the null hypothesis* when that's the wrong answer. Is this OK? There are three things we have to consider: **cost** of getting new data, the **risk** of making an incorrect decision based on this test, and the **ethical considerations** associated with someone else using our results to make *their* decisions.

- First, does it cost a lot to get more data? Not really.
- Second, what decision will I make based on this test? If I work for the marketing company, and the flavors I choose to produce will (in part) rest on the results of this test, then there's a lot at stake.
- Finally, will anyone else be using my data or analysis to make *their* decisions? Probably yes. We know that all quantitative analysis is shared among employees and managers at this marketing company, so there's always a chance.

As a result, let's instead choose an **α of 0.01,** meaning that **1 out of every 100 times** we run this test, we will *reject the null hypothesis* when that's the wrong thing to do. If we draw this conclusion, we're going to invest time, effort, and maybe money chasing a problem that doesn't exist. But by choosing this value for our level of significance, we're establishing a basis for acceptable risk: if we draw an incorrect conclusion one time we run this test every 100, that's OK.

Step 3: Calculate Test Statistic (T.S.)

This is a Chi-square test of independence, so our test statistic is a χ^2:

$$\chi^2 = \sum_{cells} \frac{(Observed - Expected)^2}{Expected}$$

We will find the value for χ^2 by using R as a calculator. First, we construct the contingency table and tack on the marginal distributions as `col.totals` and `row.totals`:

```
> lemon <- c(26,30,31,34)
> berry <- c(34,31,29,30)
> wmelo <- c(31,30,33,34)
> simple.ct <- rbind(lemon,berry,wmelo)
> col.totals <- lemon+berry+wmelo
> row.totals <- c(sum(lemon),sum(berry),sum(wmelo),sum(col.totals))
> full.ct <- rbind(lemon,berry,wmelo,col.totals)
> full.ct <- cbind(full.ct,row.totals)
> full.ct
                       row.totals
lemon        26 30 31 34      121
berry        34 31 29 30      124
wmelo        31 30 33 34      128
col.totals 91 91 93 98        373
```

We find the value for χ^2 by using the formula above. I'm going to create new variables called `expected` and `observed` so that it's easier to see how we're calculating the value of the test statistic. The expected values for each cell are found by multiplying the *row total for that cell* by the *column total for that cell*, and then dividing by the *total total* that's in the bottom right hand corner of the full contingency table.

```
> expected <- c( ((121*91)/373), ((121*91)/373), ((121*93)/373), ((121*98)/373),
((124*91)/373), ((124*91)/373), ((124*93)/373), ((124*98)/373),
((128*91)/373), ((128*91)/373), ((128*93)/373), ((128*98)/373) )
> observed <- c( 26,30,31,34,   34,31,29,30,   31,30,33,34 )
> chi.sqrd <- sum(  ((observed-expected)^2)/expected  )
> chi.sqrd
[1] 1.500775
```

Step 4: Draw a Picture

The value of χ^2 that we calculated is approximately $\chi^2=1.5$. Before we draw the picture, we need to know the degrees of freedom which we calculate using `df = (rows-1)(cols-1)`. Since we have 3 rows and 4 columns, df = 2 x 3 = 6. The area in the right tail will be very, very large.

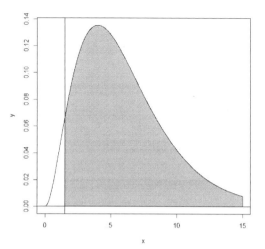

Here is the code that produced that plot:

```
> x <- seq(0,15,0.01)
> y <- dchisq(x, df=6)
> plot(x,y,type="l")
> abline(v=+1.5)
> abline(h=0)
> which(x=="1.5")
[1]  151
> length(x)
[1]  1301
> 1501-151+1
[1]  1351
> polygon(c(x[151:1501],rev(x[151:1501])), c(rep(0,1351),rev(y[151:1501])),
col="lightgray")
```

Our p-value is going to be maybe 90-98%. There's no way we're going to reject our null hypothesis.

Step 5: Calculate P-Value

From Step 4, we estimated that the total shaded area (our P-value) will be about zero. Now let's find out exactly how large the shaded area is. Since pchisq finds the area to the left, we have to subtract from 1 to get the area to the right:

```
> 1-pchisq(1.5,df=6)
[1] 0.9594946
```

The area to the right of our calculated test statistic is approximately 95.9%.

Step 6: Draw Conclusion

Is the P-Value < α? If so, reject the null hypothesis (H₀).

Is 0.959 < 0.01? **Not by a long shot.** We **fail to reject** the null hypothesis (H₀) that flavor preference and age group are independent. *One group does not overwhelmingly prefer one flavor.*

Step 7: Construct a Confidence Interval & Double Check in R

There is no confidence interval for this test, however, you can create confidence intervals on one proportion (e.g. the % of preferring eco-friendly packaging) or the difference between proportions e.g. (% of observations in each income category that prefer each of the packaging types).

We can also run the test in R to see if we've calculated our test statistic and p-value correctly. We call `chisq.test` on the contingency table that contains *just* the raw data (without the totals in the margins), using `correct=FALSE`. (Although it looks like we're telling R to get the wrong answer, what we're *actually* asking is that Yates' continuity correction is not applied.) Notice that the test statistic, the degrees of freedom, and the P-value are exactly what we calculated.

```
> chisq.test(simple.ct, correct=FALSE)

        Pearson's Chi-squared test

data:  simple.ct
X-squared = 1.5008, df = 6, p-value = 0.9594
```

Chi-Square Test of Independence: SNAP_R Phishing Utility

SNAP_R is a program written to automate the process of "spear phishing" - that is, contacting an individual online while masquerading as a "trusted source" and convincing him or her to divulge sensitive personal (or business) information. I found out about this tool watching a video from DEFCON 24, an annual hacker's conference held in Las Vegas. They provided some observations about how many times their victims clicked malicious links based on whether humans or SNAP_R were doing the phishing.

We are told that **the hackers running this test convinced 275 people out of 819 to click through,** compared to 49 out of 129 when a human was doing the phishing. **Are the method of attack and the success of the attack independent, or is there some relationship between them?**

	Human Phisher	SNAP_R Phishing Utility
Victim Escaped	80	544
Victim Compromised	49	275

Step 0: Check Assumptions

- **Random sample** - Although we don't know what sampling strategy was used, we will assume that the sample is random. ✔
- **Observations are independent** - After watching the DEFCON 24 video, we are certain that the subjects did not know one another, and that one individual's response to the phishing activity did not influence others' responses. ✔
- **Sample is small enough** - Is our sample of n=948 phishing attempts less than 10% of the size of the entire population of phishing attempts? Unfortunately, yes... there are thousands of phishing attempts each day. ✔
- **At least 5 (or 10) counts per cell** - There are well over the minimum observations in each cell. ✔

Step 1: Set Null (H₀) & Alternative (Hₐ) Hypotheses:

For the Chi-square test of independence, just plug in the names of your two categorical variables to the null and alternative hypotheses:

H₀: Success of attack is independent of method of attack.
Hₐ: Success of attack is dependent upon method of attack.

The forms of the null and alternative hypotheses are always the same – we want to see if the two categorical variables are independent (or if there's something interesting going on).

Step 2: Set α, the Level of Significance:

An **α of 0.05** means that **1 out of every 20 times** we collect data to run this test, we accept that we will *reject the null hypothesis* when that's the wrong answer. Is this OK? There are three things we have to consider: **cost** of getting new data, the **risk** of making an incorrect decision based on this test, and the **ethical considerations** associated with someone else using our results to make *their* decisions.

- First, does it cost a lot to get more data? Not really, but it does take time to engage in a phishing activity with a new target, so there is a cost in terms of time and effort.
- Second, what decision will I make based on this test? If I am the perpetrator, this test might reveal to me whether I should continue to employ human hackers to manage the phishing activity. If I am an enforcement agent, this test might help me decide what interventions to invest in.
- Finally, will anyone else be using my data or analysis to make *their* decisions? Probably yes. In fact, if this information is made public, it's likely that other threat actors will see it online and make decisions about whether *they* should write phishing software.

As a result, let's instead choose an **α of 0.01,** meaning that **1 out of every 100 times** we run this test, we will *reject the null hypothesis* when that's the wrong thing to do. If we draw this conclusion, we're going to invest time, effort, and maybe money chasing a problem that doesn't exist. But by choosing this value for our level of significance, we're establishing a basis for acceptable risk: if we draw an incorrect conclusion one time we run this test every 100, that's OK.

Step 3: Calculate Test Statistic (T.S.)

This is a Chi-square test of independence, so our test statistic is a χ^2:

$$\chi^2 = \sum_{cells} \frac{(Observed - Expected)^2}{Expected}$$

We will find the value for χ^2 by using R as a calculator. First, we construct the contingency table and tack on the marginal distributions as `col.totals` and `row.totals`:

```
> escaped <- c(80,544)
> compromised <- c(49,275)
> ct <- rbind(escaped,compromised)  # Contingency Table (without margins)
> col.totals <- escaped+compromised
> row.totals <- c(sum(escaped),sum(compromised),sum(escaped)+sum(compromised))
> full.ct <- rbind(escaped,compromised,col.totals)
> full.ct <- cbind(ct,row.totals)   # Contingency Table (with margins)
> full.ct
                   row.totals
escaped       80 544        624
compromised   49 275        324
col.totals   129 819        948
```

We will find the value for χ^2 by. I'm going to create a new variable called observed so that it's easier to see how we're calculating the value of the test statistic.

```
> expected <- c( ((624*129)/948), ((624*819)/948), ((324*129)/948), ((324*819)/948) )
> observed <- c( 80, 544, 49, 275 )
> chi.sqrd <- sum(  ((observed-expected)^2)/expected  )
> chi.sqrd
[1] 0.962124
```

Step 4: Draw a Picture

The value of χ^2 that we calculated is approximately $\chi^2=0.96$. We draw a Chi-square distribution with one degree of freedom (which looks like an exponential curve), calculated as `df=(rows-1)(cols-1)`. The picture shows the area we will be trying to find in Step 5, which is less than half, so maybe 30-40%:

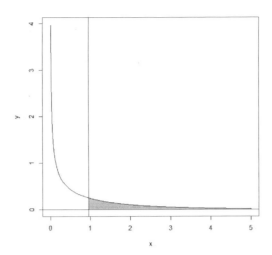

Here's the code that produced this plot:

```
> x <- seq(0,5,0.01)
> y <- dchisq(x, df=1)
> plot(x,y,type="l")
> abline(v=+0.96)
> abline(h=0)
> which(x=="0.96")
[1] 97
> length(x)
[1] 501
> 501-97+1
[1] 405
> polygon(c(x[97:501],rev(x[97:501])), c(rep(0,405),rev(y[97:501])), col="lightgray")
```

Step 5: Calculate P-Value

From Step 4, we estimated that the total shaded area (our P-value) will be 30-40%. Now let's find out exactly how large the shaded area is. Since pchisq finds the area to the left, we have to subtract from 1 to get the area to the right:

```
> 1-pchisq(0.962,df=1)
[1] 0.3266835
```

The area to the right of our calculated test statistic is approximately 32.7%.

Step 6: Draw Conclusion

Is the P-Value < α? If so, reject the null hypothesis (H₀).

Is 0.327 < 0.01? **No.** We **fail to reject** the null hypothesis (H₀) that the success of an attack is dependent upon whether there is a human or automated software program managing the phishing attempt.

Step 7: Construct a Confidence Interval & Double Check in R

There is no confidence interval for this test, however, you can create confidence intervals on one proportion (e.g. the % of a successful attack) or the difference between proportions (% success from a human phisher versus % success from the software phisher).

We can, however, run the test in R to see if we've calculated our test statistic and p-value correctly. We call `chisq.test` on the contingency table that contains *just* the raw data (without the totals in the margins), using correct=FALSE. (Although it looks like we're telling R to get the wrong answer, what we're *actually* asking is that Yates' continuity correction is not applied.) Notice that the test statistic, the degrees of freedom, and the P-value are exactly what we calculated.

```
> chisq.test(my.ct, correct=FALSE)

        Pearson's Chi-squared test

data:  my.ct
X-squared = 0.96212, df = 1, p-value = 0.3267
```

Chi-Square Goodness-of-fit Test: College Ages

A university with an enrollment of a little over 45,000 people randomly sampled its students for their ages. The ages of 9396 students were distributed like this:

Up to 18	19	20	21	22 +
1607	2102	2305	1992	1390

Are students' ages uniformly distributed?

Step 0: Check Assumptions

- **Random sample** – Although we don't know *how* the sampling was performed, we are told that the sample is random. ☑
- **Observations are independent** – There is no reason to think the values are related to other values, or that there are covariates we haven't identified. ☑
- **No "Structual Zeroes"** – There can't be a cell that contains a possibility that's physically impossible. The example I like the best is for a 2x2 contingency table where gender is one categorical variable, and ovarian cancer is the other. Since males cannot have ovarian cancer, this cell would contain a "structural zero". ☑
- **No Quantitative Variables** – This test works best when there is no required order to the categories. Although it *can* be applied for distributions of continuous variables, the way in which you bin the data becomes important, and alternative tests (e.g. Anderson-Darling or Kolmogorov-Smirnov) perform better. ☑
- **Expected Cell Frequencies > 5** – When you calculate your expected frequencies, you need to make sure all cells contain at least 5 expected observations. With so many observations, this will not be a problem. ☑

Step 1: Set Null (H₀) & Alternative (Hₐ) Hypotheses:

For the Chi-square goodness of fit test, the null and alternative hypotheses are:

H_0:   The data are consistent with the specified distribution.
H_a: The data are *not* consistent with the specified distribution.

The forms of the null and alternative hypotheses are always the same – we want to see if the data comes from the distribution we think it does.

Step 2: Set α, the Level of Significance:

An **α of 0.05** means that **1 out of every 20 times** we collect data to run this test, we accept that we will *reject the null hypothesis* when that's the wrong answer. Is this OK? There are three things we have to consider: **cost** of getting new data, the **risk** of making an incorrect decision based on this test, and the **ethical considerations** associated with someone else using our results to make *their* decisions.

- First, does it cost a lot to get more data? Not really, but it does take time to engage in a phishing activity with a new target, so there is a cost in terms of time and effort.
- Second, what decision will I make based on this test? If I am the perpetrator, this test might reveal to me whether I should continue to employ human hackers to manage the phishing activity. If I am an enforcement agent, this test might help me decide what interventions to invest in.
- Finally, will anyone else be using my data or analysis to make *their* decisions? Probably yes. In fact, if this information is made public, it's likely that other threat actors will see it online and make decisions about whether *they* should write phishing software.

As a result, let's instead choose an **α of 0.01,** meaning that **1 out of every 100 times** we run this test, we will *reject the null hypothesis* when that's the wrong thing to do. If we draw this conclusion, we're going to invest time, effort, and maybe money chasing a problem that doesn't exist. But by choosing this value for our level of significance, we're establishing a basis for acceptable risk: if we draw an incorrect conclusion one time we run this test every 100, that's OK.

Step 3: Calculate Test Statistic (T.S.)

This is a Chi-square goodness of fit test, so our test statistic is a χ^2:

$$\chi^2 = \sum_{cells} \frac{(Observed - Expected)^2}{Expected}$$

We will find the value for χ^2 by using R as a calculator. First, we construct the contingency table and tack on the total in the margin. Next, we divide the total observation count by 5 (the number of options). These are our *expected values*; how many students we would expect to appear in each category if the ages were distributed uniformly across these categories.

Up to 18	19	20	21	22 +	
1872.6	1872.6	1872.6	1872.6	1872.6	9363

```
ages <- c(1607,2102,2305,1992,1390)
expected <- rep(1872.6,5)   # repeat the value 1872.6 five times
```

```
> xsq.elements <- ((ages-expected)^2)/expected
> sum(xsq.elements)
[1] 297.6058
```

Our calculated value for χ^2 is 297.61.

Step 4: Draw a Picture

The value of χ^2 that we calculated is approximately χ^2=297.61. We draw a Chi-square distribution with four degrees of freedom (which looks like an exponential curve), calculated as `df=(rows-1)(cols-1)`. This is a *huge* value for the test statistic, so our area is going to be just about zero. In the plot on the next page, the bump in the Chi-square distribution is all the way on the left-hand side, and the vertical line is drawn at χ^2=297. There is no more room left to be captured in the tail.

```
x <- seq(0,400,1)
y <- dchisq(x, df=4)
plot(x,y,type="l")
abline(v=297)
abline(h=0)
```

Step 5: Calculate P-Value

From Step 4, we estimated that the total shaded area (our P-value) will be 30-40%. Now let's find out exactly how large the shaded area is. Since `pchisq` finds the area to the left, we have to subtract from 1 to get the area to the right:

```
> 1-pchisq(297.61,df=4)
[1] 0
```

We don't even get a tiny, tiny number in scientific notation: we get zero.

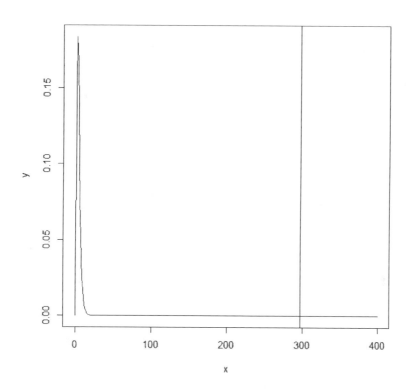

Step 6: Draw Conclusion

Is the P-Value < α? If so, reject the null hypothesis (H₀).

Is the P-Value < α? If so, reject the null hypothesis (H_o).

Is 0 < 0.01? **Yes.** We **reject** the null hypothesis (H_o) that the data comes from the specified uniform distribution. This is somewhat a surprise – if we work in admissions at this school, we may be trying to balance our class sizes, and class is typically associated with age (e.g. freshmen are 17 or 18, sophomores are 18 or 19, and so on). We'll explore the problem in a little more depth after we double check the results from our Chi-square goodness of fit test in R.

165

Step 7: Construct a Confidence Interval & Double Check in R

There is no confidence interval for this test, however, you can create confidence intervals on one proportion (e.g. the % of occurrence of a specific case, compared to the expected value). Checking your work in R is easy though:

```
> chisq.test(ages, p=c(1/5,1/5,1/5,1/5,1/5))

        Chi-squared test for given probabilities

data:  ages
X-squared = 296.44, df = 4, p-value < 2.2e-16
```

Let's plot the distribution of ages and see if we can figure out what kind of distribution it *does* come from. First, a barplot. Order the bars by lowest to highest age, and treat it as a continuous variable:

```
> barplot(ages,main="Distribution of Ages",names.arg=c("Up to 18",19,20,21,"22+"))
```

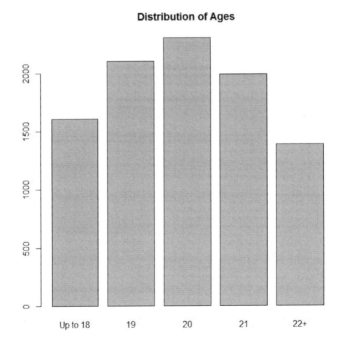

Distribution of Ages

Based on the distribution, it *looks* like it might be normally distributed. We can check this using the Shapiro-Wilk test. For this test, the null and alternative hypotheses are:

H_0:   The data are normally distributed.
H_a: The data are *not* normally distributed.

To execute the test in R, do this:

```
> shapiro.test(ages)

        Shapiro-Wilk normality test

data:  ages
W = 0.95036, p-value = 0.7398
```

This is a large P-Value, so we fail to reject the null hypothesis that the data are normally distributed. Looks like we have a normal distribution! Let's quickly do a QQ plot to visually verify:

```
> qqnorm(ages,pch=16,cex=2)
> qqline(ages,lwd=2)
```

Normal Q-Q Plot

Simple Linear Regression: Conficker Worm

Every day, the Australian Internet Security Initiative (AISI) collects data on the number of attempted malware attacks on its member organizations. In this example, we wanted to take a look at the Conficker worm, which targets the Microsoft Windows operating system (specifically, vulnerability #MS08-067) and has been observed since 2008. It allows hackers to remotely install software on targeted machines, so one defense for Windows users is to turn off the "auto-run" function which automatically runs files.

We wanted to see if Conficker infections are increasing or decreasing over time, and fit a linear trend line to our observations so we can predict (forecast) future levels of infection. This example uses data gathered from https://portal.aisi.acma.gov.au/static/data/aisi_malware_totals.csv on July 25, 2017 covering 85 days of observations from April 27 to July 20, 2017. You can get the data with this URL:

```
conficker <-
read.table("https://raw.githubusercontent.com/NicoleRadziwill/Data-for-R-
Examples/master/conficker.txt",header=TRUE)
```

Step 0: Check Assumptions

- **Observations are independent** – There is no reason to think the number of Conficker infections on one day depend on the number of infections on another day. ✅
- **Error terms are independent** – We'll have to check this after we generate the fit. If there are patterns in our residuals, then a linear fit is not appopriate.
- **Relationship between variables is linear** – We did a quick plot of our data, and it appeared to be linear, so we think a linear model might be appropriate. ✅
- **Values for the response variable are normally distributed around the mean of the response** – Again, this is something we have to check *after* our linear model is constructed. The distribution of the residuals should be normal.
- **Homoscedasticity** – The variance of the response variables should be approximately the same regardless of what x-neighborhood you look at. When we looked at the initial scatterplot, we didn't see a megaphone pattern, so this assumption checks out. ✅

Step 1: Set Null (H₀) & Alternative (Hₐ) Hypotheses:

To test the significance of the slope and the intercept for a linear model, the null and alternative are:

H_0:   The slope of the best-fit line is zero.
H_a: The slope of the best-fit line is nonzero.

H_0:   The intercept of the best-fit line is zero.
H_a: The intercept of the best-fit line is nonzero.

The forms of the null and alternative hypotheses are always the same – we want to see if our slope is a significant predictor, and if our intercept is significant on its own. The significance of the slope is more important than the significance of the intercept. When a slope is not significant, that means the independent variable that corresponds to that slope is not a significant predictor. But when an intercept is not significant, you usually would not remove it from the model because you're forcing the model to say that the response will be zero when all the predictors are zero.

Additionally, the value we're comparing the slope and intercept to *doesn't have to be zero*. We could test against the null hypothesis that the slope is a particular value, or that the intercept is a particular value – and in this case, we would adjust the numerator of the test statistic by *subtracting off* that new, nonzero value on the right-hand side of the null hypothesis. For this example, we compare to zero.

Step 2: Set α, the Level of Significance:

An **α of 0.05** means that **1 out of every 20 times** we collect data to run this test, we accept that we will *reject the null hypothesis* when that's the wrong thing to do. Is this approach OK for this regression case? There are three things we consider: **cost** of getting new data, the **risk** of making an incorrect decision based on this test, and the **ethical considerations** associated with someone else using our results to make *their* decisions.

- First, does it cost a lot to get more data? Not really. AISA updates their data set every day.
- Second, what decision will I make based on this test? If I find that infections are increasing, I might dedicate more resources to fighting Conficker. In addition, if the model is good, I might use it to determine whether there is anomalous Conficker activity in the future.
- Finally, will anyone else be using my data or analysis to make *their* decisions? Probably not. I'm not going to publish it, and I'm only going to use it internally for managing my own systems.

As a result, let's stick with an **α of 0.05**.

Step 3: Calculate Test Statistic (T.S.)

We calculate a test statistic t for both the slope and the intercept. In both cases, we place the *estimated value of the slope (or intercept) in the numerator,* and the *standard error of that estimate* in the denominator. First, we need a best-fit line to provide those estimates. Start by calculating the slope of the best-fit line:

$$\hat{\beta}_1 = r_{xy} \frac{s_y}{s_x}$$

This requires knowing the correlation coefficient (r_{xy}), the standard deviation of our y-coordinates (s_y) and the standard deviation of our x-coordinates (s_x). All of these are very easy to compute in R since we have our data loaded into the variable name `conficker`. Let's attach that file first to make the variable names easier to type, and then compute the estimated slope. We put extra parenthesis around the `est.beta1` calculation so that it prints the value to the screen in addition to storing it in the `est.beta1` variable:

```
> attach(conficker)
> (   est.beta1 <- cor(day,incidents)*(sd(incidents)/sd(day))   )
[1] -0.5130741
> mean(day)   # mean of our x coordinates
[1] 43
> mean(incidents)
[1] 777.7882 # mean of our y coordinates
> sd(day)
[1] 24.6813   # standard deviation of our x coordinates
> sd(incidents)
[1] 93.40747 # standard deviation of our y coordinates
```

Now we can estimate the intercept by remembering that all best-fit lines go through the point represented by (average of x, average of y).

$$\bar{y} = \beta_0 + \beta_1 \bar{x}$$

$$\beta_0 = \bar{y} - \beta_1 \bar{x}$$

$$\beta_0 = 777.7882 - (-0.5131)(43) = 799.8515$$

Finally, insert the estimates for the slope and intercept back into the original equation, and we have the equation for our best-fit line:

$$y = 799.852 - 0.5131x$$

The standard error of our estimated slope is calculated like this:

$$SE(\hat{\beta}_1) = \frac{S_e}{\sqrt{SS_{xx}}}$$

$$S_e = \sqrt{\frac{\sum Residuals^2}{n - 2}}$$

$$SS_{xx} = \sum(x_i - \bar{x})^2$$

Let's start with the bottom calculation of the sum of squares for our x's. To get this term, we add up the squared deviations between the x-coordinates of our data points and the average of all the x's. The extra parenthesis tell R to print the computed value as it's storing it into the variable `ss.xx`:

```
> (   ss.xx <- sum((day-mean(day))^2) )
[1] 51170
```

Calculating s_e is a little tricky, since we have to compute the difference between every data point we have and the fitted (predicted) value of that data point. We're going to cheat a little bit, and ask R to generate a best-fit model for us so we can access the entire array of residuals (`model$residuals`) for the fitted model:

```
> model <- lm(conficker$incidents ~ conficker$day)
> se <- sqrt((sum((model$residuals^2)) /  (length(day)-2)))
```

Now we have all the variables we need to compute the standard error of the estimated slope:

```
> (se.slope <- se / sqrt(ss.xx))
[1] 0.4115724
```

The test statistic t is obtained by dividing the estimate of the slope by the standard error:

$$t = \frac{\hat{\beta}_1}{SE(\hat{\beta}_1)} = \frac{-0.5131}{0.4116} = -1.247$$

Now let's find the value of the test statistic for our intercept. The format is exactly the same as for the slope: we divide our estimate of the intercept by the standard error of that estimate. So all we need to do before we're able to solve for t is figure out the standard error of the estimated intercept. Even though the intercept is β_0 in our equation above, let's call it alpha (α) so we don't get it confused with the other beta (the slope):

$$SE(\alpha) = s_e \sqrt{\frac{\sum x^2}{n \, SS_{xx}}}$$

```
> se*sqrt(sum(day^2)/(85*ss.xx))
[1] 20.37595
```

And finally, find the test statistic t for the intercept:

$$t = \frac{\alpha}{SE(\alpha)} = \frac{799.852}{20.376} = 39.21$$

Step 4: Draw a Picture

We don't need to draw a picture for our intercept test – that test statistic t is *huge*, and it's going to be so far out on the tail that we know our P-Value will be zero. But we *should* draw a picture for the test on the slope. Even though this is a t-test, we'll use the normal distribution as an approximation since our sample size is pretty big:

```
> x <- seq(-4,4,0.01)
> y <- dnorm(x)
> plot(x,y,type="l")
```

```
> abline(h=0)
> abline(v=-1.25)
> abline(v=+1.25)
> which(x=="-1.25")
[1] 276
> which(x=="1.25")
[1] 526
> polygon(c(x[1:276],rev(x[1:276])), c(rep(0,276),rev(y[1:276])), col="lightgray")
> polygon(c(x[526:801],rev(x[526:801])), c(rep(0,276),rev(y[526:801])),
col="lightgray")
```

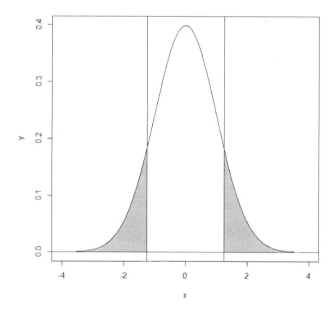

Step 5: Find the P-Value

Using the 68-95-99.7 Rule, we know that the area is a little less than what's in the tails beyond $z=-1$ and $z=+1$ (100%-68%=32%). We estimate that the P-Value for the slope test will be around 0.25. The exact value is:

```
> pt(-1.247,df=84) * 2
[1] 0.2158633
```

Step 6: Draw Conclusion

Is the P-Value < α? If so, reject the null hypothesis (H₀).

For the slope: Is 0.216 < 0.05? **No.** We **fail to reject** the null hypothesis (H₀) that the slope of the regression line is nonzero.

For the intercept: Is 0 < 0.05? **Yes.** We **reject** the null hypothesis (H₀) that the intercept is zero.

Step 7: Construct a Confidence Interval & Double Check in R

There is a confidence interval *for every single data point* so it would be very stressful to do it all by hand. Let's use the `plot.add.ci` function to make it easier:

```
> source("https://raw.githubusercontent.com/NicoleRadziwill/R-
Functions/master/plotaddci.R")
> plot(day,incidents,pch=16,cex=2)
> abline(model,lwd=2,col="red")
> plot.add.ci(day,incidents,interval="confidence",level=0.95,lwd=3,col="blue")
```

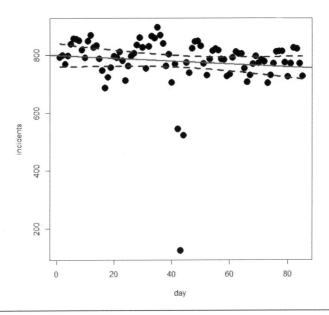

A couple of things are evident from this plot: 1) we have a few outliers, and 2) most of our points fall outside the 95% confidence interval. It's not surprising that the slope was not significant. Let's take a look at our model details in R:

```
> model <- lm(conficker$incidents ~ conficker$day)
> summary(model)

Call:
lm(formula = conficker$incidents ~ conficker$day)

Residuals:
    Min      1Q  Median      3Q     Max
-654.79  -25.02   14.09   46.57  114.11

Coefficients:
              Estimate Std. Error t value Pr(>|t|)
(Intercept)   799.8504    20.3760  39.255   <2e-16 ***
conficker$day  -0.5131     0.4116  -1.247    0.216
---
Signif. codes:  0 '***' 0.001 '**' 0.01 '*' 0.05 '.' 0.1 ' ' 1

Residual standard error: 93.1 on 83 degrees of freedom
Multiple R-squared:  0.01838,    Adjusted R-squared:  0.006553
F-statistic: 1.554 on 1 and 83 DF,  p-value: 0.216
```

First, you should notice *lots of familiar values* in this output. All values in the `Estimate`, `Std. Error`, `t value` and `Pr(>|t|)` columns are the same as those we calculated analytically for both the slope and intercept cases! Next, we see that the `Adjusted R-squared` value is 0.006, meaning that less than 1% of the variation in the data is captured by our model. That's not great! Our data has far more variability than we can capture in this linear model.

We should also examine our residuals. The charts on the next page, which were generated by plot(model), indicate that there is no discernible pattern in the residuals. This is good – it tells us that a linear fit is not inappropriate.

What else could we do to potentially improve our model and make it useful as a forecast tool? The linear model we've developed is *not* useful. One possibility is to drop outliers. (I'm not a fan of this approach, but it is sometimes used.) In the bottom two plots, we can see that data points 42, 43, and 44 are outliers. Maybe we can check to see if there was something going wrong on those days – perhaps not all the malware infections were reported. If that is indeed the case, then we could drop those outliers and try to build the model again (unfortunately, this doesn't improve the Adjusted R-Squared very much at all). Another approach would be to try time series modeling, perhaps using exponential smoothing or Autoregressive Integrated Moving Averages (ARIMA).

```
> par(mfrow=c(2,2))
> plot(model)
```

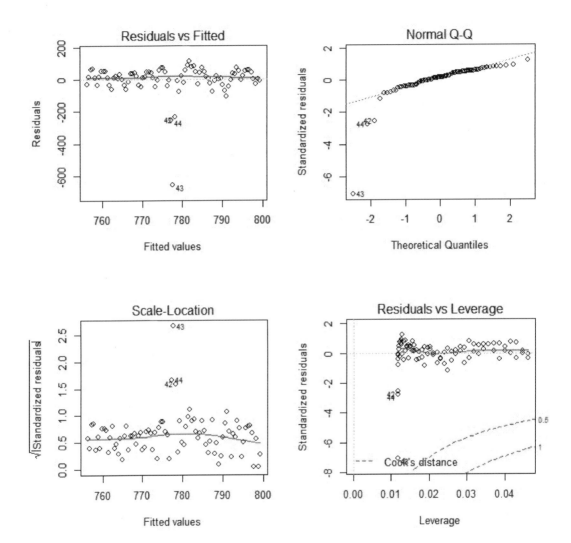

Multiple Linear Regression: Beer Foam

A person's perception of the quality of beer is based, in part, on the character and "mouthfeel" of the foamy head that forms when the beer is poured into a glass. There's a whole science around this! One of my students decided to test four different varieties of beer to understand the relationship between foam structure and perceived quality.

We wanted to see if we could predict the half-life of the foam (`tau`) from the variables we could measure: poured beer height (`beer.ht`), height of the wet, thick foam (`wet.foam.ht`), height of the drier top foam (`dry.foam.ht`), and ratio between dry and wet foam layers (`dry.foam.ratio`). We suspected that there *would be* a relationship because the taller the foam height, the more stable the foam tends to be, and the more solid the mouthfeel. If we discovered a relationship, this would mean that (for the type of beer we were analyzing) the height of the foam (when poured) could be used as a proxy for perceived quality. You can get a subset of this data (one product only) with this code:

```
foam <- read.csv("https://raw.githubusercontent.com/NicoleRadziwill/Data-for-
R-Examples/master/beer-foam.csv",header=TRUE)

brcold <- foam[foam$test.case=="3B-COLD",]
```

Step 0: Check Assumptions

- **Observations are independent** – My student took special care to make sure his study was set up so that the results from one pour would not influence the results from any other pour. ☑
- **Error terms are independent** – We'll have to check this after we generate the fit. If there are patterns in our residuals, then a linear model would not be appropriate.
- **Relationship between variables is linear** – We did a quick plot of our data for each of the variables using `pairs(foam)`, and several appeared to be linear, so we think a linear model might be appropriate. ☑
- **Values for the response variable are normally distributed around the mean of the response** – Again, this is something we have to check *after* our linear model is constructed. The distribution of the residuals should be normal.
- **Homoscedasticity** – The variance of the response variables should be approximately the same regardless of what x-neighborhood you look at. When we looked at the initial scatterplots of the data, we didn't see any megaphone or related patterns, so this assumption checks out. ☑

Step 1: Set Null (Hₒ) & Alternative (Hₐ) Hypotheses:

To test the significance of the slope and the intercept for a linear model, the null and alternative are:

H₀: The slope of the best-fit line is zero.
Hₐ: The slope of the best-fit line is nonzero.

H₀: The intercept of the best-fit line is zero.
Hₐ: The intercept of the best-fit line is nonzero.

The forms of the null and alternative hypotheses are always the same – we want to see if our slope is a significant predictor, and if our intercept is significant on its own. **For a multiple regression model (with more than one independent variable) we test the slope hypothesis for *each* predictor, but only once for the intercept.** That's because the multiple regression model has one slope term β_n for each of n predictors, but only one intercept term β_0:

$$y = \alpha + \beta_1 x_1 + \beta_2 x_2 + \beta_3 x_3 + \ldots + \beta_k x_k + \epsilon$$

The significance of the slope is more important than the significance of the intercept. When a slope is not significant, that means the independent variable that corresponds to that slope is not a significant predictor. But when an intercept is not significant, you usually would not remove it from the model because you're forcing the model to say that the response will be zero when all the predictors are zero. Additionally, the value we're comparing the slope and intercept to *doesn't have to be zero*. We could test against the null hypothesis that the slope is a particular value, or that the intercept is a particular value – and in this case, we would adjust the numerator of the test statistic by *subtracting off* that new, nonzero value on the right-hand side of the null hypothesis. For this example, we compare to zero.

Step 2: Set α, the Level of Significance:

An **α of 0.05** means that **1 out of every 20 times** we collect data to run this test, we accept that we will *reject the null hypothesis* when that's the wrong thing to do. Is this approach OK for this regression case? There are three things we consider: **cost** of getting new data, the **risk** of making an incorrect decision based on this test, and the **ethical considerations** associated with someone else using our results to make *their* decisions.

- First, does it cost a lot to get more data? Yes. Each pour requires us to buy one more beer.

- Second, what decision will I make based on this test? If we can create a good model for tau, we'll stop measuring it directly – and that will save us money in the future.
- Finally, will anyone else be using my data or analysis to make *their* decisions? Probably not.

As a result, let's stick with an **α of 0.05**.

Steps 3 through 7

Performing calculations analytically is not as straightforward for multiple regression as it is for simple linear regression, although the steps are the same. As a result, we'll skip the analytical steps and only solve this problem in R. The test statistic is computed by taking the ratio of the estimate to the standard error of the estimate:

$$t = \frac{\alpha}{SE(\alpha)}$$

$$t = \frac{\beta_n}{SE(\beta_n)}$$

Now that you know this relationship, you should easily spot the relationships in the R output:

```
> model4 <- lm(tau ~ wet.foam.ht + beer.ht + dry.foam.ht + dry.foam.ratio)
> summary(model4)

Call:
lm(formula = tau ~ wet.foam.ht + beer.ht + dry.foam.ht + dry.foam.ratio)

Residuals:
    Min      1Q  Median      3Q     Max
-22.926  -7.908   1.725   7.219  24.808

Coefficients:
                 Estimate Std. Error t value Pr(>|t|)
(Intercept)    -1317.587    183.218  -7.191 2.17e-08 ***
wet.foam.ht       86.057     11.033   7.800 3.66e-09 ***
beer.ht           42.339      8.098   5.228 8.04e-06 ***
dry.foam.ht      -93.879     12.819  -7.323 1.47e-08 ***
dry.foam.ratio  1177.251    186.552   6.311 3.02e-07 ***
---
Signif. codes:  0 '***' 0.001 '**' 0.01 '*' 0.05 '.' 0.1 ' ' 1

Residual standard error: 12.45 on 35 degrees of freedom
Multiple R-squared:  0.9549,    Adjusted R-squared:  0.9498
F-statistic: 185.3 on 4 and 35 DF,  p-value: < 2.2e-16
```

Take any value in the `Estimate` column and divide by the corresponding entry in the `Std.Error` column, and you'll get the `t value`. Based on the magnitude of the `t value`, you can tell approximately how tiny the P-Value `Pr(>|t|)` will be using an estimate based on the 68-95-99.7 Rule.

The model that we developed has one response variable (`tau`) and four independent predictor variables (`wet.foam.ht`, `beer.ht`, `dry.foam.ht`, and `dry.foam` ratio). Based on the P-Values, *each one of these terms is a significant predictor.* The equation of the model is:

$$\tau = 86.057(wet.foam.ht) + 42.339(beer.ht) - 93.879(dry.foam.ht)$$

$$+1177.251(dry.foam.ratio) - 1317.587$$

Is this a good model? In addition to each of the predictors (and the intercept) being significant, the Adjusted R-squared tells us that 94.98% of the variability in the data is captured by the model. *This is really good.* But ultimately, we want to develop a *parsimonious* regression model (that is, using the fewest number of predictors as possible to prevent *overfitting*). Can we build a model that keeps the Adjusted R-squared high, but uses fewer variables? Let's try building a few of them:

```
model3 <- lm(tau ~ wet.foam.ht + beer.ht + dry.foam.ratio)
model2a <- lm(tau ~ beer.ht + dry.foam.ratio)
model2b <- lm(tau ~ wet.foam.ht + beer.ht)
model1 <- lm(tau ~ wet.foam.ht)
```

We can list the characteristics of each model using the `summary` command:

```
> summary(model3)

Call:
lm(formula = tau ~ wet.foam.ht + beer.ht + dry.foam.ratio)

Residuals:
    Min      1Q  Median      3Q     Max
-37.844 -12.346  -2.473  11.050  46.099

Coefficients:
                Estimate Std. Error t value Pr(>|t|)
(Intercept)     -786.150    263.972  -2.978  0.00516 **
wet.foam.ht       10.903      6.358   1.715  0.09495 .
beer.ht            1.074      9.126   0.118  0.90698
dry.foam.ratio   982.615    289.728   3.392  0.00170 **
---
```

```
Signif. codes:  0 '***' 0.001 '**' 0.01 '*' 0.05 '.' 0.1 ' ' 1

Residual standard error: 19.53 on 36 degrees of freedom
Multiple R-squared:  0.8858,    Adjusted R-squared:  0.8763
F-statistic:  93.1 on 3 and 36 DF,  p-value: < 2.2e-16


> summary(model2a)

Call:
lm(formula = tau ~ beer.ht + dry.foam.ratio)

Residuals:
   Min    1Q Median    3Q    Max
-30.99 -13.99  -5.52  11.28  48.24

Coefficients:
                Estimate Std. Error t value Pr(>|t|)
(Intercept)      -340.40      47.25  -7.204 1.52e-08 ***
beer.ht             6.64       8.75   0.759 0.452775
dry.foam.ratio    545.33     141.13   3.864 0.000434 ***
---
Signif. codes:  0 '***' 0.001 '**' 0.01 '*' 0.05 '.' 0.1 ' ' 1

Residual standard error: 20.04 on 37 degrees of freedom
Multiple R-squared:  0.8765,    Adjusted R-squared:  0.8698
F-statistic: 131.3 on 2 and 37 DF,  p-value: < 2.2e-16


> summary(model2b)

Call:
lm(formula = tau ~ wet.foam.ht + beer.ht)

Residuals:
    Min     1Q  Median     3Q     Max
-26.473 -17.789  -6.517  12.423  56.520

Coefficients:
             Estimate Std. Error t value Pr(>|t|)
(Intercept)    51.364    105.683   0.486  0.62982
wet.foam.ht    -8.073      3.420  -2.360  0.02364 *
beer.ht        23.933      6.972   3.433  0.00149 **
---
Signif. codes:  0 '***' 0.001 '**' 0.01 '*' 0.05 '.' 0.1 ' ' 1

Residual standard error: 22.13 on 37 degrees of freedom
Multiple R-squared:  0.8493,    Adjusted R-squared:  0.8412
F-statistic: 104.3 on 2 and 37 DF,  p-value: 6.203e-16
```

```
> summary(model1)

Call:
lm(formula = tau ~ wet.foam.ht)

Residuals:
   Min     1Q Median     3Q    Max
-33.32 -21.81  -4.09  20.30  54.18

Coefficients:
            Estimate Std. Error t value Pr(>|t|)
(Intercept)  410.967     15.832   25.96  < 2e-16 ***
wet.foam.ht  -18.869      1.524  -12.38 6.57e-15 ***
---
Signif. codes:  0 '***' 0.001 '**' 0.01 '*' 0.05 '.' 0.1 ' ' 1

Residual standard error: 25.07 on 38 degrees of freedom
Multiple R-squared:  0.8014,    Adjusted R-squared:  0.7961
F-statistic: 153.3 on 1 and 38 DF,  p-value: 6.572e-15
```

With three predictors, the Adjusted R-Squared is 0.8763; with two predictors, 0.8698 and 0.8412; and with one predictor, it is 0.7961. All of these are reasonably good models (using Adjusted R-squared as our basis). We should look at other factors to decide which model to use operationally, for example: which variables are the *easiest* to collect? Which variables are the *cheapest* to collect? Since any of the models may be useful in practice, we need to turn to considerations like these for model selection. Note that the intercept is significant in all cases.

Notice how we 1) started with all possible predictors and stepped *down* to one fewer predictors with each new model, and 2) we used Adjusted R-squared as the basis for determining which models were good and which were unacceptable. This is a stepwise regression approach. You can also step *up* and start with one variable, then gradually add variables until performance levels off.

Similarly, you can use information *other than* the Adjusted R-squared to make your decision, including Mallow's Cp, the Akaike Information Criterion (AIC), and Schwarz's Bayesian Information Criterion (BIC). The `leaps` package in R lets you perform exploratory regression model selection using all of these criteria and both forwards and backwards stepwise approaches.

Chi-Square Test for One Variance: Conficker Worm

Every day, the Australian Internet Security Initiative (AISI) collects data on the number of attempted malware attacks on its member organizations. In this example, we wanted to take a look at the Conficker worm, which targets the Microsoft Windows operating system (specifically, vulnerability #MS08-067) and has been observed since 2008. It allows hackers to remotely install software on targeted machines. A stable process will be centered about a mean, and have a stable variance. As a result, one way to tell if the circumstances that influence a process are changing is to examine a sample of data, and compare its variance to a historical (or target) variance. Variance is related to standard deviation like this (I remember it by putting them in alphabetical order from left to right, then putting a square root sign on the right-hand side):

$$SD = \sqrt{Variance}$$

The historical variance associated with Conficker incidents was determined by our organization to be 1300. We wanted to see if the data over the most recent 10-day period demonstrated this pattern, so we pulled data from https://portal.aisi.acma.gov.au/static/data/aisi_malware_totals.csv. You can get the data with this URL:

```
conficker <-
read.table("https://raw.githubusercontent.com/NicoleRadziwill/Data-for-R-
Examples/master/conficker.txt",header=TRUE)

recent <- conficker[75:85,]$incidents
```

Step 0: Check Assumptions

- **Random sample** – Our sample doesn't look random because we're testing the past 10 days worth of data. However, the AISI organization collects only a sample of the reported incidents across Australia. We can consider this to be a random sample. ☑
- **Observations are independent** – We believe that there is no relationship between the number of attacks in subsequent days. ☑
- **Observations are normal or nearly normal** – We constructed a quick histogram using `hist(recent,col="lightgray")` which is shown on the next page. It appears to be nearly normal. Just to be sure, we also did a QQ plot which corroborated this conclusion using `qqnorm(recent);qqline(recent)`. ☑

Histogram of recent

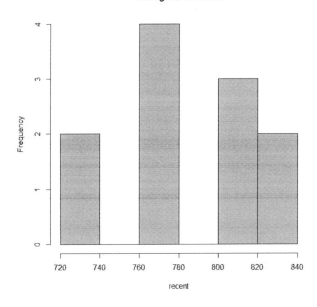

Normal Q-Q Plot

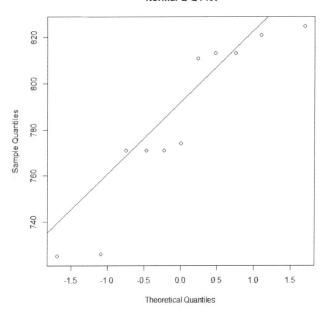

Step 1: Set Null (H₀) & Alternative (Hₐ) Hypotheses:

To test the sample variances against a standard, target, or recommended value σ_0^2, the null and alternative are:

H₀:	$\sigma^2 = \sigma_0^2$	
Hₐ:	$\sigma^2 > \sigma_0^2$	(one-tailed test)
	$\sigma^2 < \sigma_0^2$	(one-tailed test)
	$\sigma^2 \neq \sigma_0^2$	(two-tailed test)

The value you choose for σ_0^2 *can* be zero, but is often a standard, target, or baseline for a process. For our worm example, we will set these null and alternative hypotheses with σ_0^2 at 1300 based on the information that we were given by our organization.

H₀:	$\sigma^2 = 1300$	(variance in the incidents is what we expect)
Hₐ:	$\sigma^2 > 1300$	(variance is *too high...* there is more variability than we expect)

Step 2: Set α, the Level of Significance:

An **α of 0.05** means that **1 out of every 20 times** we collect data to run this test, we accept that we will *reject the null hypothesis* when that's the wrong thing to do. Is this approach OK for a variance test? There are three things we consider: **cost** of getting new data, the **risk** of making an incorrect decision based on this test, and the **ethical considerations** associated with someone else using our results to make *their* decisions.

- First, does it cost a lot to get more data? Yes. In addition to having to wait for additional days to pass, the data itself is pretty damaging: we're tracking malware attacks.
- Second, what decision will I make based on this test? We will use this test to determine whether the attack pattern is the same as historically expected, or different. If the variance pattern changes, the "popularity" of the worm may be changing, and we want to be able to detect such a shift.
- Finally, will anyone else be using my data or analysis to make *their* decisions? No.

As a result, let's stick with an **α of 0.05**.

Step 3: Calculate Test Statistic (T.S.)

This is a Chi-square test so our test statistic is a χ^2:

$$\chi^2_{df} = \frac{(n-1)s^2}{\sigma_0^2} = \frac{(n-1) \; x \; Sample \; Variance}{Reference \; or \; Target \; Variance}$$

We can plug in the information from our dataset in R to calculate this, adding outer parentheses to force R to display the value on the screen in addition to saving it in the `ts.xsq` variable:

```
> (ts.xsq <- ((length(recent)-1) * var(recent)) / 1300)
[1] 9.932448
```

Step 4: Draw a Picture

Let's draw a Chi-square distribution with 9 degrees of freedom and shade everything from χ^2=9.9 all the way to the right to mark out the right tail:

```
x.grid = seq(0,100,length=100)
dens.all = dchisq(x.grid,df=9)
x.above <- x.grid[x.grid>9.9]
dens.above <- dens.all[x.grid>9.9]
plot(dens.all,type="l",lwd=2)
polygon(c(x.above,rev(x.above)),c(rep(0,length(x.above)),rev(dens.above)),col=
"black",density=40)
```

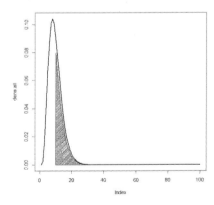

Step 5: Find the P-Value

The area looks pretty big – maybe half of everything under the whole distribution. The exact value is:

```
> pchisq(ts.xsq, df=(length(recent)-1), lower.tail=FALSE)
[1] 0.4464398
```

Notice that we used the argument `lower.tail=FALSE`. We also could have expressed this as `1-pchisq(ts.xsq,df=9)` and omitted the final argument. The exact value (44.6%) is very close to our estimate ("maybe half").

Step 6: Draw Conclusion

Is the P-Value < α? If so, reject the null hypothesis (H$_o$).

For the slope: Is 0.446 < 0.05? **No.** We **fail to reject** the null hypothesis (H$_o$) that the variance matches the historical variance of 1300. This means we can sleep easier (sort of) – we're getting attacked according to the same pattern that we've been attacked in the past.

Step 7: Compute Confidence Interval & Double Check in R

The expression for the confidence interval is:

$$\frac{(n-1)s^2}{\chi^2_{upper}} \leq \sigma^2 \leq \frac{(n-1)s^2}{\chi^2_{lower}}$$

Unlike other confidence intervals, we just plug in the values to each side. But first we have to find χ^2_{Upper} and χ^2_{Lower}:

```
> qchisq(0.975,df=10)   # this is xsq.upper
[1] 20.48318
> qchisq(0.025,df=10)   # this is xsq.lower
[1] 3.246973
```

Finally, plug the values in to the expression:

```
> (10 * var(recent)) / 20.4832
[1] 630.3791
> (10 * var(recent)) / 3.247
[1] 3976.65
```

We are 95% confident that the real variance is between 630.34 and 3976.75. (Note that if we wanted to find a different confidence level, we would replace the first value in parenthesis on the right-hand side of our χ^2_{Upper} and χ^2_{Lower} calculations. For 99% CI, for example, the numbers would be 0.995 (marking off the upper tail) and 0.005 (marking off the lower tail).

Finally, we need to double check our calculations in R. Load the Chi-square test for variances in:

```
source("https://raw.githubusercontent.com/NicoleRadziwill/R-
Functions/master/chisqvar.R")
```

And call the function with our data:

```
> chisq.var(length(recent),var(recent),1300,alternative="greater")
$chisq.upper
[1] 20.48318

$chisq.lower
[1] 3.246973

$ts
[1] 9.932448

$cint
[1]   630.3798 3976.6831

$p.value
[1] 0.4464398

$verbose
[1] "We are 95% confident that the true [population variance] is between 630.37983 and
3976.68311."
```

The calculations match what we got analytically, and the confidence interval contains our baseline of 1300. We are well within the range of the historical variance.

F Test for Homogeneity of Variances: PVC Pipe

We produce 6" lengths of PVC pipe with a diameter of 1.3" using an extrusion process. In addition to control charting to make sure our production process stays in control, we also check to make sure that (on average) the physical parameters are meeting our specifications. We got a new machine, and we want to make sure that its performance is *at least as good* as our old machine (hopefully it will be better, but we'll worry about that at a later time). We examine the variance of the diameters, which is related to the standard deviation (SD):

$$SD = \sqrt{Variance}$$

Using a random sample of the PVC pipes from both machines, we want to know: **Is the variance of diameters for PVC pipes the same for both machines?**

```
pvc1 <-
c(1.301,1.299,1.287,1.302,1.303,1.300,1.297,1.296,1.301,1.299,1.298,1.304,1.302,1.297,
1.298,1.299,1.299,1.297,1.304,1.303,1.301,1.300,1.298,1.299,1.296,1.302,1.298,1.302,1.
300,1.303,1.299,1.297,1.296,1.304,1.300,1.301,1.299,1.297,1.298,1.301,1.301,1.299)

pvc2                                                                              <-
c(1.302,1.298,1.297,1.303,1.304,1.299,1.296,1.296,1.30,1.31,1.302,1.303,1.299,1.297,1.
298,1.299,1.3,1.296,1.297,1.303,1.305,1.30,1.299,1.299,1.298,1.298,1.3,1.303,1.302,1.2
96,1.295,1.295,1.295,1.294,1.294,1.293)
```

Copy and paste the data above into your R session to follow along with the example.

Step 0: Check Assumptions

- **Random sample** – Our sample doesn't look random because we're testing the past 10 days worth of data. However, the AISI organization collects only a sample of the reported incidents across Australia. We can consider this to be a random sample. ✔
- **Observations are independent** – We believe that there is no relationship between the number of attacks in subsequent days. ✔
- **Observations are normal or nearly normal** – We constructed a quick histogram which is shown on the next page. It appears to be nearly normal. Just to be sure, we also did QQ plots which corroborate that conclusion. *This test is very sensitive to departures from normal.* ✔

```
par(mfrow=c(1,2))
hist(pvc1,col="lightgray");hist(pvc2,col="lightgray")
```

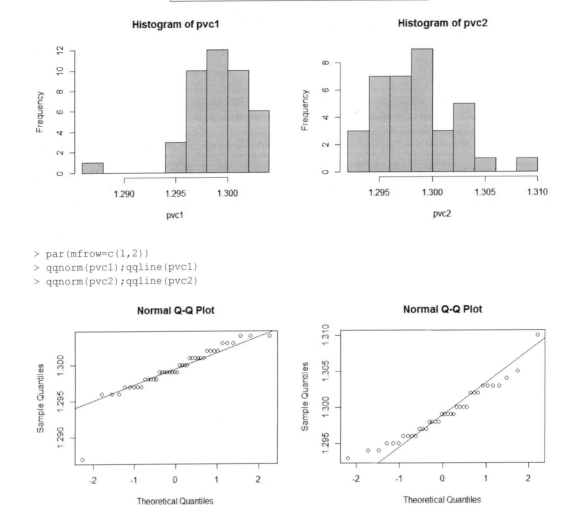

```
> par(mfrow=c(1,2))
> qqnorm(pvc1);qqline(pvc1)
> qqnorm(pvc2);qqline(pvc2)
```

Step 1: Set Null (H₀) & Alternative (Hₐ) Hypotheses:

To test the sample variances against each other, the null and alternative are:

H_0: $\sigma_1^2 = \sigma_2^2$

H_a: $\sigma_1^2 > \sigma_2^2$ (one-tailed test)

          $\sigma_1^2 \neq \sigma_2^2$ (two-tailed test)

The only important rule of thumb to remember for this test is that you should make group 1 the one with the bigger variance. **But notice**: There are only TWO options for the alternative hypothesis here!! <u>If you put the bigger variance on top *by convention*, you will never have a case where the alternative hypothesis has a "less than" sign in it</u>. For the PVC pipe case, we choose the two-tailed test. We don't care if one variance is bigger than the other, we just want to know if they are different.

Step 2: Set α, the Level of Significance:

An **α of 0.05** means that **1 out of every 20 times** we collect data to run this test, we accept that we will *reject the null hypothesis* when that's the wrong thing to do. Is this approach OK for this regression case? There are three things we consider: **cost** of getting new data, the **risk** of making an incorrect decision based on this test, and the **ethical considerations** associated with someone else using our results to make *their* decisions.

- First, does it cost a lot to get more data? It's not terribly expensive, but it's not cheap either. It also takes time to go to the factory floor, select the parts, and measure them.
- Second, what decision will I make based on this test? There's a lot riding on this test – if the new machine has a significantly different or larger variance than the old machine, we may need to get it repaired. If it's really not performing well, we may need to have it hauled away and get a new one. Not only is this a costly process, but the extrusion machine weighs nearly three tons, and moving it requires us to halt our production process.
- Finally, will anyone else be using my data or analysis to make *their* decisions? No.

As a result, let's go to an **α of 0.01**. We don't want to make major decisions about using or not using this new piece of equipment unless we're absolutely sure it's not performing the way we need it to.

Step 3: Calculate Test Statistic (T.S.)

This is an F test so our test statistic is a F:

$$F = \frac{Larger\ Variance}{Smaller\ Variance}$$

Let's calculate the test statistic for our PVC pipe data. I'm multiplying by a million since the numbers are so tiny – this will wash out in the calculation of the ratio. I just want you to see which group has a bigger variance (which is not as easy to see when the output is in scientific notation):

```
> (v2 <- var(pvc2)*1000000)
[1] 13.22778
> (v1 <- var(pvc1)*1000000)
[1] 9.131823
> v2/v1
[1] 1.448536
```

The value of our test statistic F is 1.4485.

Step 4: Draw a Picture

Let's draw an F distribution with (41,35) degrees of freedom and shade everything beyond F=1.4485:

```
> x <- seq(0,3,0.1)
> y <- df(x,df1=41,df2=35)
> plot(x,y,type="l",lwd=2)
> which(x=="1.4")
[1] 15
> length(x)
[1] 31
> polygon(c(x[15:31],rev(x[15:31])), c(rep(0,17),rev(y[15:31])), col="lightgray")
```

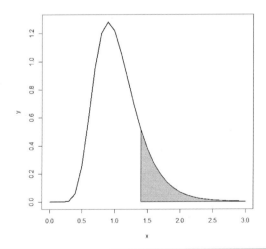

It looks like about a quarter of the area under the curve is shaded... definitely a big enough P-Value for us to *fail to reject* the null hypothesis.

Step 5: Find the P-Value

Since we have computed a test statistic F, we can look up the P-Value as long as we know the *degrees of freedom of the numerator* (that's n_1-1, or one less than the sample size of the first group) and the *degrees of freedom of the denominator* (that's n_2-1, or one less than the sample size of the second group).

Since I have 42 pipe measurements in the first group, that means my degrees of freedom for the numerator is 41. I have 36 measurements for the second group, so my degrees of freedom for the denominator is 35.

```
> length(pvc1)
[1] 42
> length(pvc2)
[1] 36
```

We will use the *rejection region* approach to solve this problem. That means we need to find the "cutoff point" beyond which calculated F values will suggest that we reject the null hypothesis. The cutoff value at which 5% of the area under the curve is in the tail is:

```
> qf(0.95,41,35)
[1] 1.731297
```

This means that if our calculated test statistic is *bigger than* 1.731, we should reject the null.

Step 6: Draw Conclusion

Is our calculated test statistic F > the critical value for F? If so, reject the null hypothesis (H_0).

Is 1.4485 > 1.7312? **No.** We **fail to reject** the null hypothesis (H_0) that the variances are different. Looks like our new machine's performance – even though the variances are slightly bigger – is just fine and (at least according to this test) we have nothing to worry about.

Step 7: Compute Confidence Interval & Double Check in R

The expression for the confidence interval is:

$$\frac{s_1^2}{s_2^2} F_{lower} \leq \frac{\sigma_1^2}{\sigma_2^2} \leq \frac{s_1^2}{s_2^2} F_{upper}$$

Unlike other confidence intervals, we just plug in the values to each side. But first we have to find F_{Upper} and F_{Lower}:

```
> qf(0.975,df1=41,df2=35)  # UPPER
[1] 1.927096
> qf(0.025,df1=41,df2=35)  # LOWER
[1] 0.527658
```

Because the ratio of variances is 1.4485, the confidence interval becomes:

$$(1.4485)\,(0.52766) \leq \frac{\sigma_1^2}{\sigma_2^2} \leq (1.4485)\,(1.9271)$$

$$0.7643 \leq \frac{\sigma_1^2}{\sigma_2^2} \leq 2.791$$

We are 95% confident that the true ratio of variances is between 0.7643 and 2.791. So they *might* be equal (with a ratio of 1), but the variance in our second machine *could be* up to three times the magnitude of the variances of PVC diameter in our first machine. It's not statistically interesting, but this may be cause for concern – we should check to see what kinds of decisions we've made in the past.

Finally, we can ask R to compute everything for us to check our analytical results. We use `var.test`, and provide the bigger variance first (to comply with convention):

```
> var.test(pvc2,pvc1)

        F test to compare two variances

data:  pvc2 and pvc1
F = 1.4485, num df = 35, denom df = 41, p-value = 0.2535
alternative hypothesis: true ratio of variances is not equal to 1
```

```
95 percent confidence interval:
 0.7643318 2.7914678
sample estimates:
ratio of variances
          1.448536
```

The test statistic F is what we expected, the P-Value looks like what we estimated, and the confidence level bounds are exactly what we expected. The P-Value is *not tiny*, so we fail to reject our null hypothesis that the ratio of the variances is 1. Our second machine appears to be performing similarly to our original machine.

Appendix A: List of Variables and Acronyms

Here are the variables and acronyms that have appeared in this text, along with a description of what they represent whenever appropriate.

Variable	What it represents
α	The level of significance for hypothesis tests. Indicates what amount of risk you are willing to incur regarding false positives; for example, $\alpha = 0.05$ indicates that 1 out of every 20 times you collect a sample and run a particular inference test, you will be rejecting the null hypothesis when you really shouldn't have (that is, reporting a false positive).
API	Application Programming Interface. Helps us use software functions that other people have written, so that we can more easily interface with their systems.
β	Coefficients in an equation for a regression model OR the proportion of false negatives in a hypothesis test. In the first case, these variables often have subscripts (β_1, β_2, etc.) to help you distinguish them from one another.
C	Contingency coefficient. Describes the strength of association between two categorical variables.
CDF	Cumulative Distribution Function. Tells us the proportion of observations in a distribution that are less than or equal to a particular value.
CSV	Comma separated values. A file format that's easy to load into R. You can save your Excel (.xls and .xlsx) files as CSV.
D_0 or d_0	In tests for the difference between means or the difference between proportions, this is the value on the right-hand side of the null hypothesis that represents the nonzero difference we're comparing our observed difference to.
$\bar{d}$	A sample statistic: In a paired t-test, d-bar represents the mean of the *differences* between pairs in your two groups.
df	Degrees of freedom. Often, it's one less than the number of items in your sample, but it's calculated differently for things like contingency tables.
ε	The error term in regression equations.
e	A mathematical constant, approximately equal to 2.71828.
erf	The error function. A special mathematical construct that appears in the definition of some probability distributions.

F	A test statistic used for ANOVA and equality of variance tests. In ANOVA, it is computed by taking the Mean Square Between groups (MSB) and dividing by the Mean Square Within (MSW) groups. In the equality of variance test, it is the ratio of the variances between the two samples you are comparing (the bigger one should always go on top).
H_0	The null hypothesis.
H_a	The alternative hypothesis.
IQR	The interquartile range, or distance between Q1 and Q3. Represents where the middle 50% of the values in the distribution are located.
JSON	JavaScript Object Notation. A data format that makes it easier to encapsulate information as objects. Many online data archives provide their information in this format.
m	The slope of the regression line.
ME	Margin of Error. Represents one half of the size of the "net" that's the confidence interval, and computed by multiplying the standard error by a critical z or critical t.
n	*A sample statistic*: the number of items in your sample
$N(\mu,\sigma)$	This refers to the normal model with a mean of μ and a standard deviation of σ
μ	*A population parameter*: the mean of a quantitative variable
μ_0	*A population parameter*: the value you are assuming that the mean of a quantitative variable. Usually appears on the right-hand side of the null and alternative hypothesis.
π	3.14159... or, sometimes, how statistics textbooks will refer to the population parameter p. (Not in this one.)
PDF	Probability Density Function. Tells us the proportion of observations we can expect to have a particular value.
p	*A population parameter*: the true proportion of some characteristic ("successes") that is present in the complete population. These values can have subscripts (1, 2, etc.) if more than one group is being compared.
$\hat{p}$	*A sample statistic*: the proportion of some characteristic ("observed successes") that is observed in your sample. These values can have subscripts (1, 2, etc.) if more than one group is being compared.
P-Value	The area underneath a probability distribution in a particular region, typically in one or both tails.
Q1	The first quartile of a distribution. 25% of the values will be below this point, and 75% will be above.
Q3	The third quartile of a distribution. 75% of the values will be below

	this point, and 25% will be above.
q	*A population parameter*: the true proportion of some characteristic ("failures") that is present in the complete population. These values can have subscripts (1, 2, etc.) if more than one group is being compared.
$\hat{q}$	*A sample statistic*: the proportion of some characteristic ("observed failures") that is observed in your sample. These values can have subscripts (1, 2, etc.) if more than one group is being compared.
r	Correlation coefficient. Tells us the strength and direction of the linear relationship between two variables.
R^2	Coefficient of determination. Tells us what proportion of the variation in a linear regression model is explained by the model (the rest is contained in the residuals).
$SE(\bar{y})$	Standard error of one mean. There is a formula used to compute this.
$SE(\bar{y}_1 - \bar{y}_2)$	Standard error of the difference between two means. There is a formula used to compute this.
$SE_{pooled}(\bar{y}_1 - \bar{y}_2)$	The pooled standard error of the difference between two means. It's a simplification of the standard error that we can get away with *if* the two groups that produced the means have approximately the same variance.
$SE(\hat{p})$	Standard error of one proportion.
$SE(\hat{p}_1 - \hat{p}_2)$	Standard error of the difference between two proportions. There is a formula used to compute this.
S_p	The pooled standard deviation used in the computation of the test statistic t for the two-sample t-test with equal variances.
s	*A sample statistic*: the standard deviation of the values in a sample, characterizing the dispersion of all the values
s^2	*A sample statistic*: the variance of the values in a sample, characterizing the dispersion of all the values in the sample.
S_x	Standard deviation of all of the x-coordinates in a dataset of (x,y) points.
S_y	Standard deviation of all of the y-coordinates in a dataset of (x,y) points.
S_{xy}	The covariance of coordinates in a dataset of (x,y) points.
σ	*A population parameter*: The standard deviation, characterizing the dispersion of all values in the population.
σ^2	*A population parameter*: The variance, characterizing the dispersion of all values in the population.
t	A test statistic that is computed for t-tests.
t^*_{df}	Critical t, which depends on the degrees of freedom (n-1) in your

	sample. Used as a scaling factor to determine the width of a confidence interval for means tests.
V	Cramer's V. Describes the strength of association between two categorical variables.
χ^2	Chi-square. A distribution (and test statistic) used to perform certain hypothesis tests.
x	*A sample statistic*: one of the quantitative values in your sample. Used to compute a z score for that value.
$\bar{x}$	*A sample statistic*: the mean of the quantitative variables within a sample. Also called the "sample mean".
$\bar{y}$	*A sample statistic*: the mean of the quantitative variables within a sample. Also called the "sample mean".
z (or z-score)	When using the normal model, z represents the number of standard deviations above or below the mean. It is also the test statistic that is computed for z-tests.
z*	Critical z. The z score that corresponds to a particular area under the normal distribution, used as a scaling factor to determine the width of a confidence interval for proportions tests. For 90% CI z*=1.645, for 95% CI z*=1.96, and for 99% CI z*=2.58.

Appendix B: Finding Critical Values and P-Values

You have a/an...	You want to find...	How you get it
Area (or P-Value)	The **z-score** that is located at the position on the horizontal axis where that area is contained *to the left* of the z-score under the normal curve	`qnorm(`**`area`**`)`
Area (or P-Value)	The **z-score** that is located at the position on the horizontal axis where that area is contained *to the right* of the z-score under the normal curve	`qnorm(1-`**`area`**`)`
Area (or P-Value)	The **t-score** that is located at the position on the horizontal axis where that area is contained *to the left* of the t-score under the t distribution (must know degrees of freedom df)	`qt(`**`area`**`,df=`**`df`**`)`
Area (or P-Value)	The **t-score** that is located at the position on the horizontal axis where that area is contained *to the right* of the z-score under the t distribution (must know degrees of freedom df)	`qt(1-`**`area`**`,df=`**`df`**`)`
Area (or P-Value)	The **F value** that is located at the positive on the horizontal axis where that area is to the *left* in the ***lower tail*** (must know number of degrees of freedom df for both numerator and denominator)	`qf(`**`area`**`,`**`df`**$_{num}$`,`**`df`**$_{den}$`)`
Area (or P-Value)	The **F value** that is located at the positive on the horizontal axis where that area is to the *right* in the ***upper tail*** (must know number of degrees of freedom df for both numerator and denominator)	`qf(1-`**`area`**`,`**`df`**$_{num}$`,`**`df`**$_{den}$`)`

Area (or P-Value)	The $\chi 2$ **value** that is located at the position on the horizontal axis where that area is contained *to the left* of that χ^2 value under the Chi-square distribution (must know degrees of freedom `df`)	`qchisq(`**`area`**`,df=`**`df`**`)`
Area (or P-Value)	The $\chi 2$ **value** that is located at the position on the horizontal axis where that area is contained *to the right* of that χ^2 value under the Chi-square distribution (must know degrees of freedom `df`)	`qchisq(1-`**`area`**`,df=`**`df`**`)`
Desired **size for the confidence interval** (CI% expressed as a decimal, e.g. 0.95)	**Critical z** (or z*)	`qnorm(`**`CI`**`+((1-`**`CI`**`)/2))`
Desired **size for the confidence interval** (CI% expressed as a decimal) *and* the number of degrees of freedom df	**Critical t** (or t*df)	`qt(`**`CI`**`+((1-`**`CI`**`)/2), df=`**`df`**`)`
x or y	The **area (P-Value)** under the normal curve to the *left* of that x or y value, and you know the `mean` and the standard deviation `sd` of the distribution they come from	`pnorm(`**`x`**`,`**`mean`**`,`**`sd`**`)`
x or y	The **area (P-Value)** under the normal curve to the *right* of that x or y value, and you know the `mean` and the standard deviation `sd` of the distribution they come from	`1-pnorm(`**`x`**`,`**`mean`**`,`**`sd`**`)`
χ^2	The **area (P-Value)** under the Chi-square distribution to the *left* of that	`pchisq(`**`chisq`**`,df=`**`df`**`)`

	χ^2 value (must know degrees of freedom df)	
χ^2	The **area (P-Value)** under the Chi-square distribution to the *right* of that χ^2 value (must know degrees of freedom df)	`1-pchisq(`**`chisq`**`, df=`**`df`**`)`
t-score	The area under the t distribution to the *left* of that t-score	`pt(`**`t`**`, df=`**`df`**`)`
t-score	The area under the t distribution to the *right* of that t-score	`1-pt(`**`t`**`, df=`**`df`**`)`
z-score	The area under the normal curve to the *left* of that z-score	`pnorm(`**`z`**`)`
z-score	The area under the normal curve to the *right* of that z-score	`1-pnorm(`**`z`**`)`

Examples

```
> # Find the area to the left of a z-score of -2
> pnorm(-2)
[1] 0.02275013
> # 2.27% of the area under the normal curve lies to the left of z=-2

> # Find the area to the left of x=2.9 in a normal model with
> # MEAN of 3.00 and a standard deviation SD of 0.01:
> pnorm(2.9,mean=3,sd=0.1)
[1] 0.1586553
> # 15.8% of the area under THIS normal curve lies to the left of x=2.9

> # Find the critical t (t*) for a 99% CI with df=9
> CI <- 0.99
> df <- 9
> qt(CI+((1-CI)/2), df=df)
[1] 3.249836
```

Appendix C: The `shadenorm.R` Function

Background

Many of the pictures of shaded areas under the normal distribution in this book were created using the `shadenorm` function, originally posted to the R Bloggers web site at http://www.r-bloggers.com/how-to-shade-under-a-normal-density-in-r/. To use it, 1) source the file into your R session using the first line of code below, 2) copy and paste the whole function below into your R session, or 3) copy and paste the whole function into a file called `shadenorm.R`, then put it into your R working directory and use `source("shadenorm.R")` to load the function into memory. An alternative to `shadenorm` is `polygon` on p. 73 and 400.

```
source("https://raw.githubusercontent.com/NicoleRadziwill/R-
Functions/master/shadenorm.R")
```

The `shadenorm` Function

```
# by Tony Cookson
# http://www.r-bloggers.com/how-to-shade-under-a-normal-density-in-r/

shadenorm = function(below=NULL, above=NULL, pcts = c(0.025,0.975), mu=0,
      sig=1, numpts = 500, color = "gray", dens = 40, justabove= FALSE,
      justbelow = FALSE, lines=FALSE, between=NULL, outside=NULL) {

    if(is.null(between)){
        below = ifelse(is.null(below), qnorm(pcts[1],mu,sig), below)
        above = ifelse(is.null(above), qnorm(pcts[2],mu,sig), above)
    }

    if(is.null(outside)==FALSE){
        below = min(outside)
        above = max(outside)
    }
    lowlim = mu - 4*sig
    uplim  = mu + 4*sig

    x.grid = seq(lowlim,uplim, length= numpts)
    dens.all = dnorm(x.grid,mean=mu, sd = sig)
    if(lines==FALSE){
        plot(x.grid, dens.all, type="l", xlab="X", ylab="Density")
    }
    if(lines==TRUE){
        lines(x.grid,dens.all)
```

```
    }

    if(justabove==FALSE){
        x.below     = x.grid[x.grid<below]
        dens.below = dens.all[x.grid<below]

polygon(c(x.below,rev(x.below)),c(rep(0,length(x.below)),rev(dens.below)),co
l=color,density=dens)
    }
    if(justbelow==FALSE){
        x.above     = x.grid[x.grid>above]
        dens.above = dens.all[x.grid>above]

polygon(c(x.above,rev(x.above)),c(rep(0,length(x.above)),rev(dens.above)),co
l=color,density=dens)
    }

    if(is.null(between)==FALSE){
        from = min(between)
        to   = max(between)

        x.between     = x.grid[x.grid>from&x.grid<to]
        dens.between = dens.all[x.grid>from&x.grid<to]

polygon(c(x.between,rev(x.between)),c(rep(0,length(x.between)),rev(dens.betw
een)),col=color,density=dens)
    }

}
```

Examples

You can use shadenorm to shade *regions between* two z-scores:

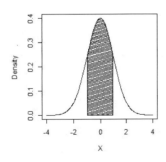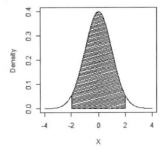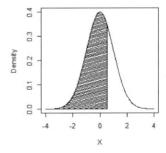

Here is the code that produced the three graphs above. Notice that the leftmost graph has the region between z=-1 and z=+1 shaded, the middle graph has the region between z=-2 and z=+2 shaded, and the rightmost graph has everything shaded from all the way in the left tail (z=-Inf) to z=0.537, about half a standard deviation above the mean. We've also chosen to change the default shading color from gray to black:

```
> par(mfrow=c(1,3))
> shadenorm(between=c(-1,+1),color="black")
> shadenorm(between=c(-2,+2),color="black")
> shadenorm(between=c(-Inf,0.537),color="black")
```

Or, you can use shadenorm to shade regions *between actual values of your own data*. For example, if you're modeling pulse rate in terms of beats per minute, and know that the mean pulse rate in a population of Americans between 18 and 24 years old is 78 beats per minute with a standard deviation of 8 beats per minute, you can use that normal model N(78,8) to create regions:

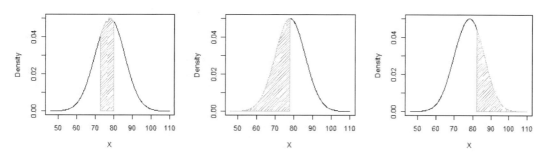

Here is the R code that created these three charts. Note that we've opted to keep the default shading color of gray:

```
> par(mfrow=c(1,3))
> shadenorm(between=c(73,80),mu=78,sig=8)
> shadenorm(between=c(-Inf,78),mu=78,sig=8)
> shadenorm(between=c(82,Inf),mu=78,sig=8)
```

Appendix D: Power Analysis and Sample Sizes

Background

Have you collected enough data for your results to be valid? You can find out by doing power analysis. Power answers the question "What's the probability that I will have enough data to know that what I *originally* thought the population was like (my null hypothesis) wasn't quite right?" If something interesting is going on in your population (that is, something *different* than your null hypothesis says) - you want to be able to catch it with your test. Typically, you want at least an 80% chance of "detecting an effect" – that is, detecting some difference from your null hypothesis – and that 80% (or 0.80) is called the *power of the test*.

Usually, you collect data once and use that collection of data to answer multiple research questions. For every research question you attempt, you need to check and make sure your sample is large enough using power analysis. If you're planning to do a one sample t-test that says you need a sample size of 58 to achieve 0.80 power, another two-sample t-test that says you need a sample size of 40 per group to achieve 0.80 power, and a one proportion z-test that says you need a sample size of 111 to achieve 0.80 power, then collect at least 111 observations and make sure that you have no less than 40 observations in each of the two groups for your two-sample t-test. You need to pick the biggest result to make sure the power of your test is large enough.

For the examples in this book, you can go back and do post-hoc power analysis to see just how effective each test was at detecting an effect – detecting a difference from the null hypothesis. (Hint: in several cases, it's under 0.80! Depending on the risk profile of each project, we might want to do back and do these studies again before making decisions that affect people's lives and well being.)

The following section is excerpted from *Statistics (The Easier Way) With R, 2nd Edition* for your convenience.

How to Conduct a Power Analysis

Clearly, having a zero percent chance of being able to use your sample to detect whether the population is unlike what you originally thought... would be bad. Similarly, having a 100% chance of being able to detect a difference would *also* probably be bad: your sample size would be comparatively large, and collecting more data is usually costlier (in both time and effort). When determining an appropriate sample size for your study, look for a power of *at least* 0.80, although higher is better; higher power is always associated with bigger sample sizes, though. The standard of 0.80 or higher just reflects that the community of researchers are usually comfortable with studies where the power is at least at this level.

The smaller the difference between what you *think* the population is like (as described by the null hypothesis) and what the *data* tells you the population is like... the more data you'll *need* to actually detect that difference. This difference between your hypothesized parameter and what the population parameter *really is* is called an **effect size**. For example, if you were trying to determine whether there was a difference between the average age of freshmen and the average age of seniors at your university, it wouldn't require such a large sample size because the *effect size* is about three years in age. However, if you were trying to determine whether there was a difference between the average age of freshmen and the average age of sophomores at your university, it would require a much larger sample size because the *effect size* is less than one year in age. If there is a difference, you will need more data in your sample to know for sure.

Effect size is represented in R as **how many standard deviations the real estimate is away from the hypothesized estimate**. Closer to zero, the effect size is small; around 0.5, the effect size becomes more significant. An effect size of 0.8 to 1 is considered large, because you're saying that the true difference between the hypothesized value of your population parameter and the sample statistic from your data is approaching one standard deviation. According to Cohen (1998) a value of 0.1 or 0.2 is a small effect size. Your job is to estimate what you think the effect size is before you perform the computation of sample size. If you really have *no way at all* of knowing what the effect size is (and this is actually a pretty common dilemma), just use 0.5 as recommended by Bausell & Li (2002).

To increase or improve your *power to detect an effect*, do one or more of these:

- **Increase your sample size**. The more items you have in your sample, the better you will have captured a snapshot of the variation throughout the population... as long as your random sample is also a representative sample.
- **Increase your level of significance**, α, which will make your test *less stringent*.
- **Increase the effect size**. Of course, this is a characteristic of your data and your a priori knowledge about the population... so this one may be really hard to change.
- **Use covariates or blocking variables**. (I won't explain this in detail; just know that if you're designing an experiment with treatment and control groups, and you need to improve your experimental design to increase the power of your statistical test, you should look into this.)

Type I Error asks:

- **How willing am I** to reject the null hypothesis when in fact, it actually pretty accurately represents what's going on with the population?
- **How willing am I** to get a false positive, where I *detected* an effect but *no effect actually exists*?
- What's the probability of **incorrectly rejecting** the null hypothesis?

This probability, the Type I Error, is the level of significance α. If you choose an α of 0.05, that means you are willing to be wrong like this 1 out of every 20 times (1/20 = 0.05) you collect a sample and run the test of inference. If you choose an α of 0.01, that means you are willing to be wrong like this 1 out of every 100 times (1/100 = 0.01) you collect a sample and run the test of inference -- making this selection of α a more stringent test. On the other hand, if you choose an α of 0.10, that means you are willing to be wrong like this 1 out of every 10 times (1/10 = 0.10) you collect a sample and run the test of inference -- making this selection of α a much less stringent test. Type I Error and Type II Error have to be *balanced* depending upon what your goals are in designing your study. Here is how they are related:

		What's really going on with the population	
		H_0 is True	**H_0 is False**
	Reject H_0	Type I Error α *FALSE POSITIVES*	**Accurate Results!** You rejected H_0 and you were supposed to, because your data showed that the population was different than what you originally thought
The decision you make as a result of your statistical test:	**Fail to Reject H_0**	**Accurate Results!** You didn't reject H_0 because it was an accurate description of the population	Type II Error β *FALSE NEGATIVES*

Power, 1 - β, is related to the Type II Error... it is:

The probability that you DON'T get a FALSE NEGATIVE

The probability that you DO detect an effect that's REAL

Process

For each of your RQs, you should have already selected the appropriate methodology for inference that you'll use to draw your conclusions. The inferential tests covered here are:

- One sample t-test
- Two sample t-test
- Paired t-test
- One-proportion z-test
- Two proportion z-test
- Chi-Square Test of Independence
- One-way Analysis of Variance (ANOVA)
- Linear Regression

All of these commands are provided by the `pwr` package, except the last one, which is in the base R installation. Be sure to install the `pwr` package first, then load it using the `library` before you start.

R Command	Statistical Methodology *(*=not covered in this chapter)*
`pwr.t.test`	One sample, two sample, and paired t-tests; also requires you to specify whether the alternative hypothesis will be one tailed or two
`pwr.t2n.test`	*Two sample t-test where the sizes of the sample from each of the two groups is different
`pwr.p.test`	One proportion z-test
`pwr.2p.test`	Two proportion z-test
`pwr.2p2n.test`	*Two proportion z-test where the sizes of the sample from each of the two groups is different
`pwr.chisq.test`	Chi-square Test of Independence
`pwr.anova.test`	Analysis of Variance (ANOVA)
`pwr.f2.test`	Linear Regression
`power.t.test`	*Another way to perform power analysis for one sample, two sample, and paired t-tests; here, the advantage is there's an easy method to plot Type I & Type II Errors & power vs. effect

Calculating Sample Sizes for Tests Involving Means (T-Tests)

This section covers sample size calculations for the one sample, two sample, and paired t-tests. You are also required to specify whether your alternative hypothesis will be one tailed or two, so be sure you have defined your H_0 and H_a prior to starting your calculations.

The `pwr.t.test` command takes *five* arguments, which means you can use it to compute power and effect size in addition to just the sample size (if you want). So the one sample t-test, we can use `pwr.t.test` like this to compute required sample size:

```
> pwr.t.test(n=NULL,sig.level=0.05,power=0.8,d=0.3,type="one.sample")

    One-sample t test power calculation

              n = 89.14936
              d = 0.3
      sig.level = 0.05
          power = 0.8
    alternative = two.sided

> pwr.t.test(n=NULL,sig.level=0.05,power=0.8,d=0.3,type="one.sample",
alternative="greater")

    One-sample t test power calculation

              n = 70.06793
              d = 0.3
      sig.level = 0.05
          power = 0.8
    alternative = greater
```

To get the sample size, we use the `n=NULL` argument to `pwr.t.test`. As expected, the one-tailed test below requires a smaller sample size than the two-tailed test above. And always round your n's up!! We can't sample an extra 0.14936 person for the first test above... we have to sample the entire person. So our correct sample size should be 90 for that test, and 71 for the test below.

We can use the same command to determine sample sizes for the two sample t-test:

```
> pwr.t.test(n=NULL,sig.level=0.05,power=0.8,d=0.3,type="two.sample",
alternative="greater")

    Two-sample t test power calculation
```

```
            n = 138.0715
            d = 0.3
    sig.level = 0.05
        power = 0.8
  alternative = greater
```

NOTE: n is number in *each* group

And the paired t-test:

```
> pwr.t.test(n=NULL,sig.level=0.05,power=0.8,d=0.3,type="paired",
alternative="greater")

     Paired t test power calculation

            n = 70.06793
            d = 0.3
    sig.level = 0.05
        power = 0.8
  alternative = greater
```

NOTE: n is number of *pairs*

Observe that you can calculate any of the values if you know *all* of the other values. For example, if you know you can only get 28 pairs for your paired t-test, you can first see what the power would be if you kept everything else the same, and then you can check and see what would happen if the effect size were just a little bigger (and thus easier to detect with a smaller sample):

```
> pwr.t.test(n=28,power=NULL,sig.level=0.05,d=0.3,type="paired",
alternative="greater")


     Paired t test power calculation

            n = 28
            d = 0.3
    sig.level = 0.05
        power = 0.4612366
  alternative = greater
```

NOTE: n is number of *pairs*

```
> pwr.t.test(n=28,power=0.8,sig.level=0.05,d=NULL,type="paired",
alternative="greater")

     Paired t test power calculation

              n = 28
              d = 0.4821407
      sig.level = 0.05
          power = 0.8
    alternative = greater

NOTE: n is number of *pairs*
```

In the first example, we used `power=NULL` to tell R that we wanted to compute a power value, given that we knew the number of pairs n, the estimated effect size `d`, the significance level of 0.05, and that we are using the "greater than" form of the alternative hypothesis. But a power of 0.46 is really not good, so we'll have to change something else about our study. If we force a power of 0.8, and instead use `d=NULL` to get R to compute the effect size, we find that using the 28 pairs of subjects we have available, we can detect an effect size that's about half a standard deviation from what we hypothesized at a power of 0.8 and a level of significance of 0.05. That's not so bad.

You can also access the sample size n directly, if that's all you're interested in, like this:

```
> pwr.t.test(n=NULL,sig.level=0.05,power=0.8,d=0.3,type="paired",
alternative="greater")$n
[1] 70.06793
```

Here is a summary of all the arguments you can pass to `pwr.t.test` to perform your sample size calculations and power analysis for tests of means:

Argument to `pwr.t.test`	What it means
n	Your sample size! Set to NULL if you want to compute it.
power	Sets the desired power level. Best to set it at 0.80 or above! But beware: the higher the desired power, the bigger your required sample size will be.
sig.level	Sets the level of significance α. Typically this will be 0.1, 0.05, or 0.01 depending upon how stringent you want your test to be (the smaller numbers correspond to more stringent tests, like you might use for high-cost or high-risk scenarios).

d	This is the effect size. A reasonable heuristic is to choose 0.1 for a small effect size, 0.3 for a medium effect size, and 0.5 for a large effect size.
`type=c(" ")`	Specify which t-test you are using: the one sample t-test (`"one.sample"`), the two-sample t-test (`"two.sample"`), or the paired t-test (`"paired"`)? Put that word inside the quotes.
`alternative=c(" ")`	Specify which form of the alternative hypothesis you'll be using... the one with the < sign (`"less"`)? The one with the > sign (`"greater"`)? Or the two-tailed test with the ≠ sign (`"two.sided"`)? Put that word inside the quotes.

Calculating Sample Sizes for Tests Involving Proportions (Z-Tests)

This section covers sample size calculations for the one proportion and two proportion z-tests. You are also required to specify whether your alternative hypothesis will be one tailed or two, so be sure you have defined your H_0 and H_a prior to starting your calculations. The `pwr.p.test` and `pwr.2p.test` commands take *five* arguments, which means you can use it to compute power and effect size in addition to just the sample size (if you want). So for the one proportion z-test, we can use `pwr.p.test` to get sample size like this:

```
> pwr.p.test(h=0.2,n=NULL,power=0.8,sig.level=0.05,alternative="two.sided")

proportion power calculation for binomial distribution (arcsine transformation)

              h = 0.2
              n = 196.2215
      sig.level = 0.05
          power = 0.8
    alternative = two.sided
```

You can access the sample size directly here as well:

```
> pwr.p.test(h=0.2,n=NULL,power=0.8,sig.level=0.05,
alternative="two.sided")$n
[1] 196.2215
```

And for the two proportion z-test, we can use `pwr.2p.test` like this to compute required sample size (or access it directly using the $n variable notation at the end):

```
> pwr.2p.test(h=0.2,n=NULL,power=0.8,sig.level=0.05,
```

```
alternative="two.sided")

     Difference  of  proportion  power  calculation  for  binomial  distribution  (arcsine
transformation)

              h = 0.2
              n = 392.443
      sig.level = 0.05
          power = 0.8
    alternative = two.sided

NOTE: same sample sizes

> pwr.2p.test(h=0.2,n=NULL,power=0.8,sig.level=0.05,
alternative="two.sided")$n
[1] 392.443
```

Here are summaries of the arguments you can pass to `pwr.p.test` and `pwr.2p.test`:

Argument to `pwr.p.test`	What it means
n	Your sample size! Set to NULL if you want to compute it.
power	Sets the desired power level. Best to set it at 0.80 or above! But beware: the higher the desired power, the bigger your required sample size will be.
sig.level	Sets the level of significance α. Typically this will be 0.1, 0.05, or 0.01 depending upon how stringent you want your test to be (the smaller numbers correspond to more stringent tests, like you might use for high-cost or high-risk scenarios).
h	This is the effect size. A reasonable heuristic is to choose 0.2 for a small effect size, 0.5 for a medium effect size, and 0.8 for a large effect size.
alternative=c(" ")	Specify which form of the alternative hypothesis you'll be using... the one with the < sign ("less")? The one with the > sign ("greater")? Or the two-tailed test with the ≠ sign ("two.sided")? Put that word inside the quotes.
Argument to `pwr.2p.test`	**What it means**
n	Your sample size! Set to NULL if you want to compute it.
power	Sets the desired power level. Best to set it at 0.80 or above! But beware: the higher the desired power, the bigger your required sample size will be.
sig.level	Sets the level of significance α. Typically this will be 0.1, 0.05, or 0.01 depending upon how stringent you want your test to

	be (the smaller numbers correspond to more stringent tests, like you might use for high-cost or high-risk scenarios).
h	This is the effect size. A reasonable heuristic is to choose 0.2 for a small effect size, 0.5 for a medium effect size, and 0.8 for a large effect size.
alternative=c(" ")	Specify which form of the alternative hypothesis you'll be using... the one with the < sign ("less")? The one with the > sign ("greater")? Or the two-tailed test with the ≠ sign ("two.sided")? Put that word inside the quotes.

Calculating Sample Sizes for the Chi-Square Test of Independence

This section covers sample size calculations for the Chi-Square Test of Independence, which is performed on a contingency table created by tallying up observations that fall in each of two categories. The purpose of this test is to determine whether the two categorical variables are *independent* or *not* (that there is *some* kind of dependency within the data; you won't be able to tell what, specifically, without further experimentation). The `pwr.chisq.test` command takes *five* arguments, and like the other tests, you can find out the value of *any* of them with the remaining values. For a 3x3 contingency table where you expect a moderate effect size and $df=(r-1)(c-1)$, you would do this:

```
> pwr.chisq.test(w=0.3,N=NULL,df=4,sig.level=0.05,power=0.8)

     Chi squared power calculation

             w = 0.3
             N = 132.6143
            df = 4
     sig.level = 0.05
         power = 0.8

NOTE: N is the number of observations
```

Argument to pwr.chisq.test	What it means
N	Your sample size! Set to NULL if you want to compute it. Note: it's a **CAPITAL N**!
power	Sets the desired power level. Best to set it at 0.80 or above! But beware: the higher the desired power, the bigger your required sample size will be.

sig.level	Sets the level of significance α. Typically, this will be 0.1, 0.05, or 0.01 depending upon how stringent you want your test to be.
w	This is the effect size. A reasonable heuristic is to choose 0.1 for a small effect size, 0.3 for medium, and 0.5 for large.
df	Degrees of freedom; calculate by taking one less than the number of rows in the table, and one less than the number of columns in the table... then multiply them together.

Calculating Sample Sizes for One-Way Analysis of Variance (ANOVA)

This section covers sample size calculations for the one-way ANOVA, which tests for equivalence between several group means, and aims to determine whether *one of these means is not like the others*. The `pwr.anova.test` command takes *five* arguments, and like the other tests, you can find out the value of *any* of them with the remaining values. For an ANOVA test with four groups, you would do this:

```
> pwr.anova.test(k=4,f=0.3,sig.level=0.05,power=0.8)

     Balanced one-way analysis of variance power calculation

              k = 4
              n = 31.27917
              f = 0.3
      sig.level = 0.05
          power = 0.8

NOTE: n is number in each group
```

Here are summaries of all the arguments you can pass to `pwr.chisq.test`:

Argument to `pwr.anova.test`	What it means
n	Your sample size, in terms of *number of observations per group*! Set to NULL if you want to compute it.
power	Sets the desired power level. Best to set it at 0.80 or above! But beware: the higher the desired power, the bigger your required sample size will be.
sig.level	Sets the level of significance α. Typically this will be 0.1, 0.05, or 0.01 depending upon how stringent you want your test to be.
f	This is the effect size. A reasonable heuristic is to choose

	0.1 for a small effect size, 0.3 for a medium effect size, and 0.5 for a large effect size.
k	Number of groups (Check the null hypothesis here... how many μ's do you see in it? That's your number of groups.)

Calculating Sample Sizes for Linear Regression

This section covers sample size calculations for regression tests, which aim to determine *whether a linear relationship exists*. The `pwr.f2.test` command takes *five* arguments, and like the other tests, you can find out the value of *any* of them with the remaining values in place. For linear regression with `k` predictors (or independent variables), and `n` pairs of observations, you set `u=k` and usually let `v=NULL` (although the expression for v is `n-(k+1)`). The last variable, `f2`, is the estimated effect size:

```
> pwr.f2.test(u=1, v=NULL, f2=0.15, sig.level=0.01, power=0.8)

     Multiple regression power calculation

             u = 1
             v = 79.23892
            f2 = 0.15
     sig.level = 0.01
         power = 0.8
```

Here are summaries of all the arguments you can pass to `pwr.2f.test`:

Argument to `pwr.2f.test`	What it means
u	The number of independent variables in the regression you want to do. For simple linear regression, u=1; for multiple regression, choose the number of factors you are using in your model.
v	Your sample size, in terms of *number of pairs of observations* - set to NULL if you want to compute it.
sig.level	Sets the level of significance α. Typically, this will be 0.1, 0.05, or 0.01 depending upon how stringent you
f2	This is the effect size. According to Cohen, 0.02, 0.15, and 0.35 represent small, medium, large effect sizes
power	Sets the desired power level. Best to set it at 0.80 or above! But beware: the higher the desired power, the bigger your required sample size will be.

Index

Made in the USA
Middletown, DE
29 August 2018